IMAGES
of America

MORRISVILLE

IMAGES
of America

MORRISVILLE

Ernest Dollar

ARCADIA
PUBLISHING

Published by Arcadia Publishing
Charleston SC, Chicago IL, Portsmouth NH, San Francisco CA

Library of Congress Catalog Card Number: 2007935335

For all general information contact Arcadia Publishing at:
Telephone 843-853-2070
Fax 843-853-0044
E-mail sales@arcadiapublishing.com
For customer service and orders:
Toll-Free 1-888-313-2665

Visit us on the Internet at www.arcadiapublishing.com

To Timmy, who introduced me to Indian Branch Hill,
and for Lesbia, who welcomed me with open arms

CONTENTS

ACKNOWLEDGMENTS

It is simply impossible to thank everyone who helped make this book. Foremost, I want to express my gratitude to all who opened their doors to me and presented their photograph albums for me to study. I have made some wonderful friends as a result, in particular Emma "Tet" Walton, Tommy Tew, Mary Jo Lumley, Dean Council, Betty Hardy, and Bob and Graham Yates. Credit for the genesis of this project belongs to town planner Benjamin Hitchings, who understands history's role in a growing community, and to the wise guidance of Prof. Craig Friend of the Department of History at North Carolina State University.

A great vote of thanks must also go to Kim Cumber of the North Carolina Office of Archives and History and to Stacie Galloway of the Town of Morrisville; to the First Baptist Church of Morrisville and the Wake County Historical Society, whose members gave much time and energy toward the success of this project; to the *News and Observer*; to the North Carolina Collection at the University of North Carolina; and to David Southern for his long hours of work. - "L.M."

INTRODUCTION

It is difficult for us today to imagine a time when the soil governed every aspect of daily life. But for the early Europeans, West Africans, and Native Americans, the success of crops and livestock was a life or death matter directly affecting everyone. In the Morrisville area, sustenance was made difficult by the quality of the earth itself. Farmers who worked the bottomlands along Crabtree Creek reaped the benefits of rich, alluvial soil, while those working higher ground suffered the curse of nutrient-poor, sandy clay formed over 200 million years ago.

Morrisville is situated at the bottom of a great, ancient pocket that stretched between today's Chapel Hill and Cary, a link in a long, waterlogged rift valley extending from New York to Georgia. The physical form of this can be observed in steep hills that enclose the Triassic Basin, a geographic feature that continues to shape Morrisville's prospects just as it has influenced Morrisville's history. The area's less-than-desirable qualities were offset by steep valley overlooks and many shallow crossings of the robust Crabtree Creek and its feeders. For at least 12,000 years, mankind has sought ways to manage and accommodate this terrain. Countless travelers wore paths through the local forests connecting points of easiest access. The town itself formed along a ridge bearing a great east-west road.

Great game animals and the Paleoindians who hunted them were the first to cut paths across Crabtree Creek at its shallow fords. These earliest Native Americans camped on the heights overlooking the future site of Morrisville, and they exploited the area's abundant natural resources. As Europeans arrived in the 1740s, they too took advantage of these natural crossings and worked the rich soil along the creek. Some of these settlers earned livings by accommodating subsequent settlers heading westward, deeper into the backcountry. Francis Jones of Edgecombe County was among the first to claim a tract of land in this area. His 1749 grant for 640 acres along Crabtree Creek was awarded by agents of John Carteret, the Earl of Granville, and Francis's son, Tignal Jones, inherited this tract after his father's death. In 1792, the new state capital of Raleigh was located at Joel Lane's massive plantation on the ridge between Crabtree and Walnut Creeks, and a year later, the cornerstone for the first building of the University of North Carolina was laid at New Hope Chapel upon the Hill. The future Morrisville community lay almost halfway between these two locations along the main road connecting them, and it was poised to prosper from the increasing traffic of the thoroughfare. The site of Morrisville, central to the developing seats of Raleigh, Pittsboro, Chapel Hill, and Hillsborough, was from its inception the heart of the Triangle.

During the American Revolution, the cash-strapped new state of North Carolina raised its operating budget through land grants. Land confiscated from those loyal to the king was sold with tracts that had remained vacant and unclaimed. The prospects for building a successful community looked bright when, in 1779, wealthy legislator Tignal Jones acquired 640 acres adjacent to his father's original tract, and on this new claim, the future town of Morrisville would develop almost a century later.

As the years passed, the promise of prosperity went unfulfilled, partly due to the unforgiving sandy soil. Neighboring centers—Raleigh as a seat of government, Durham with its booming tobacco and textile economies, and Chapel Hill as home of the University of North Carolina—grew rapidly, while Morrisville developed at a snail's pace, despite the construction of a major railroad in the 1850s and immediate proximity to a major international airport in the 1950s. The town of Morrisville benefited little from these developments until very late in the 20th century. Measured growth comes with some benefits, and it has allowed Morrisville to remain, until very recently, a rare window to the past with a pleasingly preserved community and culture.

As Morrisville races to catch up to its neighbors, much of this well-preserved world is in danger of being lost before it can be discovered and appreciated. For historians, the landscape here is rich with lore and full of new opportunities to rediscover the past. This book is likely the first to gather and retell the long history of Morrisville and its people, and it is informed by many interviews with those who still live in the area and have experienced long lives in this wonderful village. Through these photographs we are afforded an opportunity to see events, both good and bad, that were considered important enough to document on film and save for posterity. This book affords readers a unique opportunity to see through the eyes of those who have called Morrisville their home.

One

THE STRUGGLE TO LIVE
PREHISTORY–1865

Found in a local quarry, fossilized bone fragments from a pseudosuchian reptile of the late Triassic Period reveal the landscape and its inhabitants from over 200 million years ago. Then, the future site of Morrisville would have been at the bottom of the Triassic Basin, a flooded rift valley that stretched east to west between the area of present-day Cary and Chapel Hill, and south to the area of present-day Sanford. Before and after the Triassic Period, our planet suffered catastrophic geophysical events that resulted in mass extinctions. (Courtesy of Olivia Raney Library.)

These projectile points are evidence of some of Morrisville's earliest inhabitants, and they date from *c.* 8,000–6,000 BC, when large groups of nomadic proto-Americans used the future Morrisville area as a temporary camp while following game such as deer, beaver, and buffalo. (Photograph by the author.)

Settlers in the mid-18th century were attracted to the fertile land along Crabtree Creek, a major tributary of the upper Neuse River. One of the earliest land grants was awarded to Francis Jones in 1749 by agents of Lord Granville, who controlled the northern half of the colony of North Carolina. In 1779, Jones's son Tignal purchased an adjoining tract, the eventual site of Morrisville. (Photograph by the author.)

The many rivers and streams of central North Carolina also attracted settlers who understood the advantages of harnessing the motive power of swift-running streams. The Page family operated this gristmill on Crabtree Creek northwest of Morrisville. The remains of the mill can still be seen in Umstead State Park. (Courtesy of North Carolina Office of Archives and History.)

From Colonial times until the early 20th century, county officials, by way of the corvée or "road tax," assigned the important responsibility of road maintenance to the residents who lived along each route. This image from the early 1900s shows a crew at work repairing a road to Morrisville from Chatham County. (Courtesy of Betty Lou Ferrell.)

In 1771, men calling themselves Regulators attacked county court officials in Hillsborough, prompting Gov. William Tryon to march his army into the backcountry to put down the insurrection. On May 7, Tryon's army camped around the home of Tignal Jones and sent out men to arrest his neighbor, Turner Tomlinson, considered by the governor to be a "notorious Regulator." From there, the force marched westward toward the final showdown with the Regulators nine days later at the Battle of Alamance. Tryon's forces prevailed. Seven Regulators were hanged and the rest paroled, but local resistance to arrogant Colonial authority was destined to arise anew five years later with the signing of the Declaration of Independence in Philadelphia. (Courtesy of North Carolina Office of Archives and History.)

Henry and Nancy Jones were extremely prosperous, and their home between Morrisville and Raleigh, built in 1803, became an important stage stop for travelers, including Pres. James K. Polk, who visited the home in 1847. (Courtesy of North Carolina Office of Archives and History.)

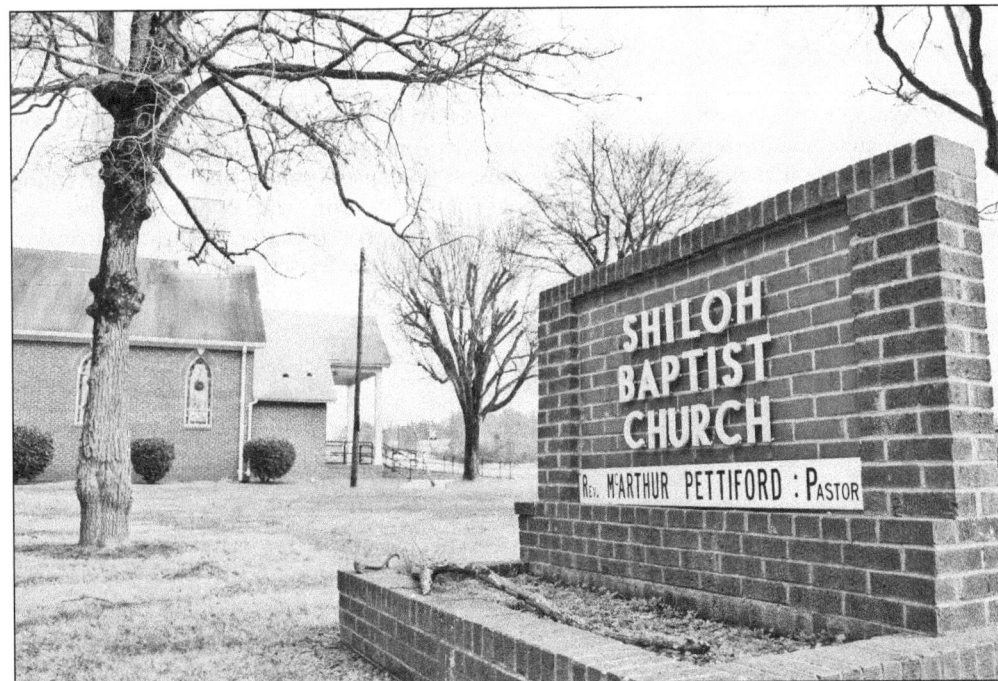

Two miles north of Morrisville lies the community of Shiloh. This area was originally settled in the late 1820s by freeborn African Americans and freed former slaves. By 1870, Shiloh had grown into a self-sufficient community with a public school, social clubs, a cooperative store, and a church. (Photograph by the author.)

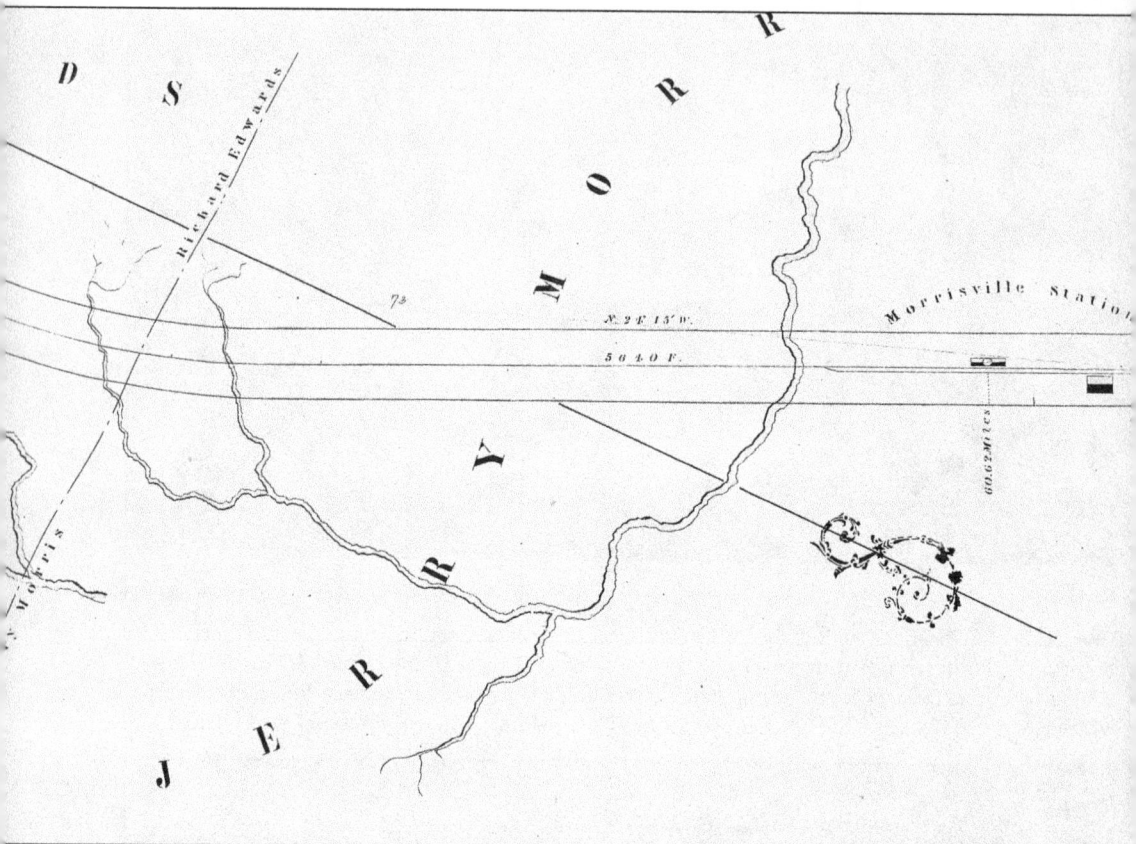

When surveyors for the North Carolina Railroad passed through Jones in 1850 seeking a location for a depot, Jeremiah Morris recognized that a wonderful opportunity had arrived at his doorstep. To locate a station at that spot was logical because of the several stagecoach roads converging there. At the Morrisville station, travelers could transfer to trains with connections east and west, and local farmers could send crops to distant markets. For decades to come, the arrival of the railroad drastically affected almost every facet of life in this developing village. (Courtesy of North Carolina Office of Archives and History.)

Jeremiah Morris lived in this house when he granted the railroad a right-of-way through his property, and he donated three acres of land for the construction of a water station, woodshed, and other buildings. After Morris's death, Williamson Page bought his home. In the final days of the Civil War, the Page family hid in the basement during a heated skirmish outside of their home, which was later occupied by Union soldiers. (Photograph by the author.)

A very young Robert D. Ferrell plays by the summer kitchen of the Williamson Page home in 1947. This kitchen and several slave cabins were razed not long after this photograph was taken. (Courtesy of Mary Jo Lumley.)

The Second Great Awakening (c. 1800–1830) inspired local residents to form the Cedar Fork Baptist Church in 1805, and it attracted many worshipers from the Morrisville community in the years before the Civil War. This image of Cedar Fork Baptist Church is from the 1930s. (Courtesy of Walter Green.)

One religious leader who especially influenced Morrisville was Methodist minister James O'Kelly. After the American Revolution, O'Kelly broke with the Methodists and formed his own denomination, establishing his first church in eastern Chatham County in 1794. O'Kelleyites merged with Congregationalists in 1931 to become the Congregational Christian Church and merged again, in 1957, with the Evangelical Reformed Church, to create the United Church of Christ. The O'Kellyite congregation of Morrisville organized on September 28, 1872, and counted several descendents of James O'Kelly among its members. They built this Gothic Revival–style church around 1900 and continued to meet in this building until the early 1970s. (Courtesy of Morrisville Town Archives.)

Upon the outbreak of the Civil War in 1861, men from the Morrisville area organized a company to fight for the Confederacy. Northern-born Sophia Partridge of Raleigh was hired to sew the blue-and-white silk banner for presentation to the men at their send-off on June 1, 1861, in the front yard of the Williamson Page house. Their flag, presented to them by the "Ladies of Cedar Fork," was inscribed with the name "North Carolina Grays." They were also referred to as the "Morrisville Grays" and later as the "Cedar Fork Rifles." (Courtesy of North Carolina Office of Archives and History.)

Williamson Page's son, Malcus Williamson Page, enlisted on May 16, 1861, and became the company's first lieutenant. Later appointed assistant quartermaster, Page was promoted to captain on October 7, 1862. For a reason now unknown, Malcus resigned his commission and left the army on April 29, 1863. After the war, he married Katherine "Kate" Clause Page, and he served Wake County as sheriff from the 1880s until 1906 and as registrar of deeds. (Courtesy of Mary Jo Lumley.)

Two brothers who enlisted in the North Carolina Grays were Quinton Isaac Hudson (left) and Thomas Hudson. This image must date from the war's first year because Thomas died of disease on December 16, 1861. Quinton also fell ill, and he was almost killed after being stabbed by a fellow soldier during an argument. After the war, Quinton returned home and became an original resident of the new town of Apex. When his children asked him about the war, he would tell his story only to break down and cry at the end of it. In 1893, Quinton was one of the pallbearers for Confederate president Jefferson Davis when his coffin passed through Raleigh. (Courtesy of David Latta.)

During the Civil War, Morrisville hosted a hospital for wounded soldiers. The town's location along the railroad and its proximity to Raleigh made it an ideal location. The North Carolina Museum of History owns this cup that was intended for patients' use. It was made by a Morrisville potter, who stamped the bottom with the identification "N.C. Hospital." (Courtesy of North Carolina Museum of History.)

Morrisville did not feel the hard hand of war until 1865. On April 13, 1865, Union cavalry captured Raleigh and fought Confederate horsemen retreating westward through Morrisville. After a skirmish between Union and Confederate cavalrymen on her farmland, Nancy Jones and a slave discovered a wounded Union soldier in her barn. They nursed him back to health, and after he returned safely home, Nancy received a gold ring in the mail from this soldier as a token of his appreciation. (Courtesy of North Carolina Office of Archives and History.)

Arriving at the heights overlooking Morrisville, Federal soldiers spied a train of several dozen cars attempting to pull away from the depot. Union artillery was ordered forward and began shelling the town. Lt. Joseph Kittinger of the 23rd New York Light Artillery commanded a section of 3-inch ordnance rifles, and he recorded the scene in his diary. "My pieces were brought forward on a run and we sent the shell in quick succession right in the midst of the retreating Johnnies, scattering them in every direction." (Courtesy of Erie and Buffalo Historical Society.)

Around midnight on April 15, 1865, Union soldiers at Morrisville were shocked to see Confederate horsemen approaching bearing a white flag and an appeal for armistice. Nine days of complicated surrender negotiations commenced at the farm of James Bennett outside Durham's Station, about 20 miles to the west. The Union commander, Maj. Gen. William T. Sherman, stopped in Morrisville several times while traveling by train to these meetings. In Morrisville, on April 17, 1865, Sherman's commanders informed him of the assassination of Pres. Abraham Lincoln. The Confederate surrender at Bennett Place, finalized on April 26 and affecting over 89,000 soldiers, was the largest of the three major surrenders that finally terminated the Civil War. (Courtesy of Library of Congress.)

Newly freed slave M. L. Latta came to Morrisville just after the end of the Civil War to conduct a school for other former slaves. He later recalled that many Freedmen thought Abraham Lincoln had sent out officials to divide up the money stored in Southern banks and would award each of them 40 acres and a mule. One woman apologized to Latta for having to miss a class because her family would be busy collecting their share of the South's riches. (Courtesy of the University of North Carolina.)

Archeological evidence suggests earthen depressions like these on Indian Branch Hill were rifle pits dug by Confederate and Union forces during the occupation of Morrisville. The randomly dug pits on the eastern side of the hill suggest a hasty construction by Confederate horsemen during the skirmish, while the well-organized pits on the western side suggest they were dug by occupying Union forces. (Photograph by the author.)

Kittinger recorded that his Federal cannoneers expended 88 rounds of ammunition during the day's fighting, but it's unknown if this total included the two live shells discovered in 1996 by boys playing in Crabtree Creek. One of these shells is currently on display in Morrisville's town hall, along with other Civil War artifacts. (Photograph by the author.)

In 1996, efforts began to preserve part of the original battlefield in Morrisville, but in 1999, development destroyed the portion of the battlefield where Federal artillery shelled the town. (Photograph by the author.)

MORRISVILLE STATION
— • • • —

On April 13, 1865, Union cavalry, under the command of General William T. Sherman, captured Raleigh and pursued the retreating Confederate cavalry west along the railroad. Rearguard skirmishes erupted at points along the Hillsborough Road until the combatants reached Morrisville. Using cavalry and artillery, Union forces attacked a Confederate train loaded with supplies and wounded. Before withdrawing, the Confederate cavalry repelled the attack long enough to allow the railcars of wounded to escape while abandoning the supplies. This was the last major cavalry engagement in Sherman's campaign. The next night, a courier from the Confederate commander, General Joseph E. Johnston, rode into the Union camp at Morrisville with a truce proposal. Subsequent negotiations between Johnston and Sherman led to the largest Confederate surrender of the Civil War at the Bennett farm in Durham on April 26.

IN MEMORY OF COMMISSIONER C.T. MOORE

In 1998, a petition to the state highway marker program for Morrisville was rejected, prompting the town to set aside funds for the signage. A year later, a private citizen paid for the sign commemorating the 1865 battle to honor town commissioner C. T. Moore. (Photograph by the author.)

Two

THE PROMISE OF
PROSPERITY
1865–1900

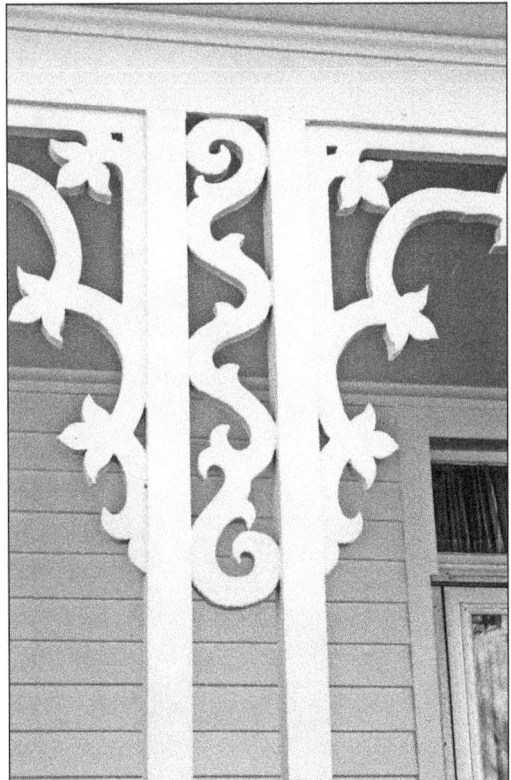

No other towns in Wake County possess more homes embellished with this style of intricate millwork. Most of these decorative elements appear on homes built or renovated between 1870 and 1880 and reflect a new sense of prosperity in the postwar years. It is believed that Page and Ellington, a local cabinet and window blind manufacturing company located in nearby Cary, created these treatments. (Photograph by the author.)

Morrisville's most visible landmark was built by James M. Pugh in 1870. Originally from Alamance County, Pugh was a prosperous Morrisville merchant as well as postmaster and justice of the peace. The gingerbread trim on his home and outbuildings reflects his new wealth and influence and is the best remaining example of the unique Morrisville decorative style. The structure stood at the corner of Aviation Parkway and North Carolina Highway 54 until it was moved in 2007. (Photograph by the author.)

Another veteran hoping to capitalize on the postwar growth was George Toonoffski, a son of a Polish immigrant who settled in Raleigh. During the Civil War, he was captured while serving as a courier for Gen. W. W. Kirkland. While in prison, Toonoffski paid another prisoner who was about to be paroled for the use of his identity. The ruse worked, and Toonoffski was released and returned home. In 1872, he opened a liquor store in Morrisville. (Courtesy of Nell Shrader.)

Bethany Church, organized in 1866, stood a short distance from Morrisville at the current intersection of Morrisville-Carpenter Road and Davis Drive. In 1874, the church decided to move into town and erect a new house of worship, and the old church was sold to the African American congregation at Shiloh. Bethany Church became Morrisville Baptist Church and was renovated in 1899. (Courtesy of First Baptist Church of Morrisville.)

Those in the Bethany Congregation who opposed the move into town founded the Good Hope Baptist Church in the Carpenter community in 1875. (Courtesy of Betty Lou Ferrell.)

The home of William and Frances Barbee was located between Bethany Church and Good Hope Baptist Church. (Courtesy of Betty Lou Ferrell.)

Morrisville's growth prompted leading citizens and businessmen to send a petition for incorporation to the general assembly on January 1, 1875. (Courtesy of Morrisville Town Archives.)

The first to sign the petition for incorporation was minister and educator William Gaston Clements. Born into poverty in the Fletcher's Chapel neighborhood in 1841, at the age of nine, Clements was put out as a hireling to work on a farm to support his family. After losing an arm in the Civil War, the self-educated Clements returned to Morrisville, where he married Annie Moring, a James O'Kelly descendant, and joined the local Christian church. He became a minister, superintendent of Wake County schools, a trustee of Elon College, and editor of the *Christian Sun*, the voice for the denomination. Clements is remembered as one of the great champions of education in Wake County and in North Carolina. (Courtesy of Emma Walton.)

The importance of Morrisville's connection to the railroad continued to grow. William H. Beasley and wife Eugenia "Jennie" Barbee moved into town, and William found employment as a section master for the railroad. The Beasleys' son, Thomas T., followed in his father's footsteps and worked on the line. In June 1902, Jennie died, and two months later, while walking on top of a moving train, Thomas was killed after slipping and falling between the cars. (Courtesy of Carlos Jordan.)

The train depot in Morrisville became an important building for residents. The town's original depot was destroyed in a 20th-century train accident. A smaller depot, seen here, was built as a replacement. (Courtesy of Morrisville Town Archives.)

The rail stop also allowed families from the surrounding community a chance to enjoy some much sought-after entertainment, and the state fair in Raleigh drew large crowds. Morrisville bustled with farmers who came into town to board the train. (Courtesy of Southern Historical Collection.)

State Fair at Raleigh.

ISSUED BY NORTH CAROLINA RAILROAD

GOOD FOR ONE PASSAGE

From *Morrisville*,

To Raleigh and Return,

ON CONDITIONS

That the passenger holding this ticket is strictly forbidden the privilege of stopping off at any point intervening the place of purchase and Raleigh.

Conductors are instructed not to recognize this Ticket after October 23d, 1877, and only then from Passengers returning getting on the train at Raleigh station.

Not Good after October 23d, 1877.

Genl. Passenger Agent

In 1879, Williamson Page built this home for his son, Sidney F. Page, and his family. The home features signature Morrisville millwork spandrels and porch. (Photograph by the author.)

John Madison Moring was born to prosperous tavern owners in the Chatham County community named after his family, Moringsville. After serving in the Civil War, Moring came to Morrisville to practice law. He was elected to the North Carolina House of Representatives in 1872 and was elected Speaker of the House in 1879. (Courtesy of Stephen Massengill.)

John Moring's brother was Morrisville merchant James M. Moring, seated here with his wife, Mary. The two sit on the front steps of the Morrisville Collegiate Institute, located adjacent to the Christian church. The school held classes on the first floor, and the Cedar Fork Masonic Lodge No. 342 met upstairs. The lodge was moved to Morrisville in 1882 but remained there only five years before relocating back to the nearby Nelson community. (Courtesy of Emma Walton.)

With the increase in business and prosperity, the means for supporting improvements in education soon followed. On July 29, 1883, the *News and Observer* reported the second commencement at Morrisville Collegiate Institute in the "quiet, healthy, and sober village." Lessie Southgate was one of the first teachers at this new school. (Courtesy of Southern Historical Society.)

When the institute closed in 1896, Morrisville's children were sent to school in Cary. In 1907, Cary High School became one of the first public high schools in North Carolina. (Courtesy of Carlos Jordan.)

Rufus Barbee and his wife, Adna, sit proudly in front of their home with their 10 sons (standing, from left to right), William, Fred, Joseph, Hubert, Sprite, Walter, Clyde, Thee, James Hal, and Hick. (Courtesy of Dean Council.)

Wagons on the main road to Raleigh would pass High House on the outskirts of Cary, a few miles east of Morrisville. These residents of High House pose for their photograph around 1897. (Courtesy of North Carolina Office of Archives and History.)

William G. Clements built this home on Church Street around 1880 for his increasing family. (Courtesy of Emma Walton.)

Stella Clements, William's daughter, was born in 1885 into a family that believed in the power of higher education, and she attended college, as did all of her siblings. This photograph of Stella is from Elon College; her father was a trustee of that college. (Courtesy of Emma Walton.)

Jack and Stella Green stand in front of their scuppernong vines in winter. In the summer months, the Green family practiced truck farming, which entailed loading up the family vehicles with produce and shopping them around to various boardinghouses and the Hayti area of Durham. (Courtesy of Emma Walton.)

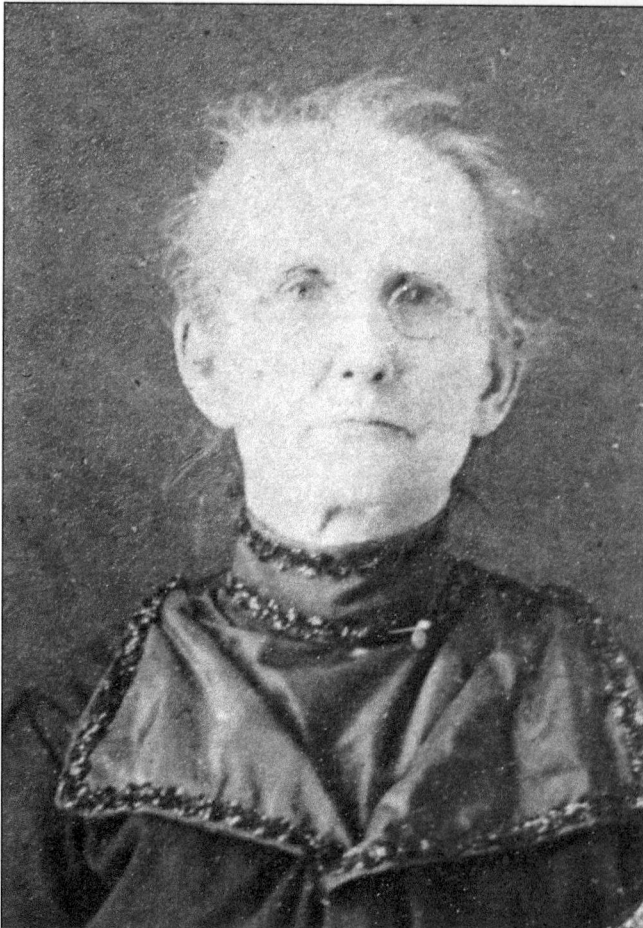

As photography became more accessible and affordable, family portraits became more commonplace. Many photographs from the late 19th and early 20th centuries are labeled with a physical description of the image on the reverse, and such is the case with this portrait of Lula Rich. On the back of the photograph is her address and the following: "Hair Black, Eyes Blue, Comp[lexion] Fair, Dress Black silk with black silk braid, gold glasses." (Courtesy of Olivia Raney Library.)

Lula Rich's daughter, Fannie, and husband, Robert, sat for photographer William Shelburn in his Durham studio sometime between 1883 and 1907. (Courtesy of Olivia Raney Library.)

Three Barbee sisters—(left to right) Minnie, Geneva, and Ida—sat for this group portrait in 1892. (Courtesy of Dean Council.)

When the United States declared war against Spain in April 1898, President McKinley issued a call for volunteers. North Carolina's initial fighting unit was the 1st North Carolina Volunteer Infantry, mustered into service on May 2, 1898, with a total of 50 officers and 932 enlisted men. On May 22, 1898, the unit received orders from the U.S. War Department to head to the front in Cuba. The noon train from Raleigh was packed with soldiers, including Morrisville native Pvt. William M. Barbee of Company I. About seven miles south of Savannah, Georgia, at 5:45 a.m., May 23, 1898, the third section of the train was struck by a freight train, killing one and injuring seven. Barbee, crushed between the cars, was killed instantly. (Courtesy of Dean Council.)

Three

A LONELY PLACE
BESIDE THE ROAD
1900–1950

Farmers gathered in 1901 under a tree on Gravel Hill outside Morrisville, and there they founded Sorrell's Grove Baptist Church. J. A. and Molly Luquire and W. H. and Nannie Arnold deeded the land to the trustees of this church on November 28, 1906. (Courtesy of Diane Lane.)

SEPARATE RECEIPT MUST BE ISSUED FOR EACH MONTH AND THE
YEAR AND MONTH FOR WHICH DUES ARE PAID MUST
BE INDICATED IN MARGIN BY PUNCH MARK

JAN. FEB. MAR. APRIL MAY JUNE JULY AUG. SEPT.

OFFICIAL RECEIPT

Brotherhood of Railroad Trainmen

No. _____ 16-17 _____ 190 6

_____ Bangor _____ LODGE No. _____

RECEIVED FROM BRO. _____ C. C. Pugh _____

DUES MONTH OF _____ 11 _____ $ 7.7 __ GEN'L GRIEVANCE COM. ASST. NO. _____ $ _____

GRAND DUES MONTH OF _____ $ .9 __ LEGISLATIVE ASST. NO. _____ $ _____

SPECIAL ASSESSMENT NO. _____ $ _____ PROTECTIVE FUND MONTH OF _____ $ _____

ADMISSION FEE _____ $ _____

_____ A. F. Newcomb _____ TOTAL _____ $ _____

FINANCIER   COLLECTOR   (Signature of Financier or Collector must be personally written)

THIS RECEIPT SHOULD NOT BEAR SEAL OF SUBORDINATE LODGE UNLESS ORDER FOR SECRET WORK ON BACK IS FILLED OUT

Cornelius Collier Pugh worked as a flagman for Southern Railroad Company. On October 18, 1906, Pugh managed to jump aboard and stop a cut of runaway cars, earning him praise from the company. During this time, Pugh joined the Brotherhood of Railroad Trainmen. On May 2, 1907, Pugh failed to protect the rear of his train with flags, resulting in a collision at Hillsborough. He was dismissed from service, but a month later, officials reinstated Pugh in light of his earlier heroism. Sadly, a year later, while backing a train, his foot became stuck and the train crushed his leg. He died on September 12, 1908, twelve hours after undergoing amputation. (Courtesy of Southern Historical Collection.)

Morrisville has surprisingly few cemeteries. Pictured is the Page family graveyard, located on their property and surrounded by an ornate iron fence. (Photograph by the author.)

The largest cemetery in Morrisville is behind the First Baptist Church (the former Morrisville Baptist Church). One plot features a rare "grave house," a small gabled shelter surrounded with a picket railing. Local lore explains that the Maynard family built the shelter because of the deceased's fear of thunder. (Courtesy of Morrisville Town Archives.)

Fannie and Alfred Morris stand in the garden of their Morrisville home. Behind them is the Morrisville Hosiery Mill, built by Samuel R. Horne in 1910 and an example of the wave of technology that was changing the Southern landscape. Beginning in the 1870s, textile mills offered poor rural families dependable jobs, reliable pay, and housing. Many turned away from farming, practiced by their ancestors for generations, and opted for the promise of the mills. Morrisville was swept up in this change with the construction of Horne's mill, which manufactured men's socks in a long, single-story structure. It was located in the lot that is now the Ruritan Park. (Courtesy of Mary Jo Lumley.)

With the influx of mill workers into Morrisville, the town's population grew; with that growth came a demand for additional housing. Horne followed the example of other mill towns like Carrboro, Durham, and Bynum by constructing housing for his workers. This house, one of the original homes built by Horne, still stands on the corner of Page and Ashe Streets. (Courtesy of Betty King Nordan.)

Despite Horne's new housing, a shortage remained, and William and Fanny Penny turned their hotel into a boardinghouse for mill workers. In 1910, their tenants included newlyweds James and Bessie Gunley, 15-year-old Bettie Stallings, and 20-year-old Sallie Myals. Young people flocked to the mill towns popping up across the Piedmont of North Carolina to earn regular wages that they could send back home to their farm families. The Penny home was destroyed in 2007. (Photograph by the author.)

William Lee Page, his wife, Clyde, and baby Mary pose with the rest of the Page family in the front yard of their home in 1911. Sons Robert (left) and William sit in front, and daughter Elizabeth stands between her parents. (Courtesy of Mary Jo Lumley.)

Another image of Clyde and Mary Page shows more of Morrisville's numerous buildings in the background. (Courtesy of Mary Jo Lumley.)

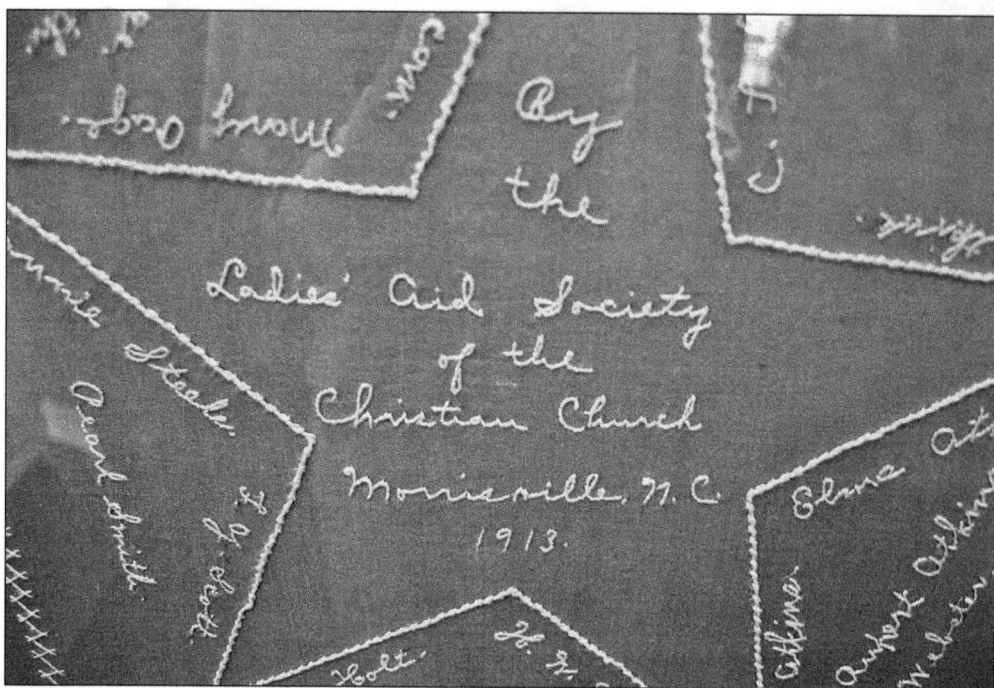

To help raise money for the Christian church, women of the congregation solicited 10¢ apiece from members to embroider their names onto a community quilt. For a few cents more, residents could get their names prominently placed in the center of a star. North Carolina governor Locke Craig was the only Baptist to have his name embroidered on the quilt. (Photograph by the author.)

Robert E. Atkins was a member of the Morrisville Baptist Church and became so moved by his faith that he was ordained its minister in 1907. Seven years later, Atkins built this one-story house with a high-pitched, pyramid-like roof across the street from the church. (Photograph by the author.)

With America's entry into World War I, several men from Morrisville were sent to fight in Europe. Before he left for war, Pvt. Richard Hilet Cotten married his 16-year-old sweetheart, Essie Godwin. (Courtesy of Betty Cotten Hardee.)

In addition to business from the railroad, Morrisville increasingly relied on the dusty automobile traffic passing through town for economic support. As cars became more prevalent and roads became more important, townspeople shifted their built environment to accommodate this new mode of transportation. In 1924, the main through road—North Carolina Highway 10, formerly the Central Highway—was paved. Shops, gas stations, and restaurants sprang up along the route to serve motorists traveling between Raleigh and Durham. Charlie Maynard's store was built before 1920 as a pharmacy and post office. In the 1930s, Bill Jones operated a grocery here before moving the operation across the railroad tracks. (Photograph by the author.)

Walter N. Searls operated another early service station in Morrisville area. Signs for Good-Grape Soda, No-Nox Motor Oil Fuel, and Gulfpride—"The Worlds Finest Motor Oil"—date the image to the late 1920s. (Courtesy of Tommy Tew.)

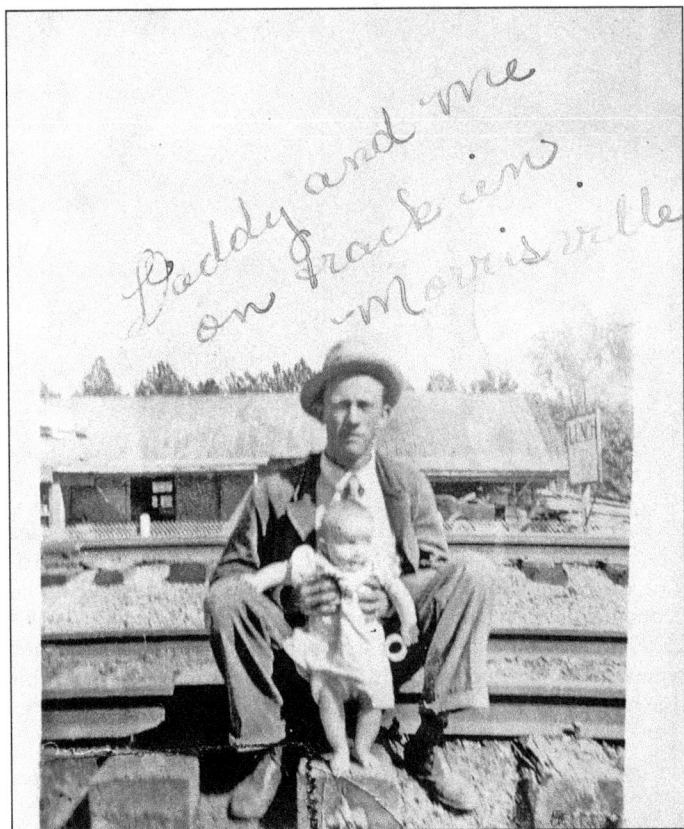

Paddy and me on track in Morrisville

Laddie Francisco, a proud new father, shows off his young daughter, Faye, in 1934. In the background is part of Morrisville's original business district. (Courtesy of Faye Francisco Godbold.)

The most dynamic minister of Shiloh Baptist Church was born a free man before the Civil War. The Reverend James Dunston was instrumental in securing land ownership, education, and economic development for residents of the Shiloh area. In 1925, Dunston personally purchased 2,000 acres of land, divided it into parcels, and offered it to families. This thriving community grew to over 57 farmers on Dunston's former property, which extended from the Durham County line to south of McCrimmon Parkway. (Photograph by the author.)

Sarah Mabel Pugh, born on November 2, 1891, was a teacher, artist, magazine illustrator, author, and composer. Mabel's father, James M. Pugh, had been a prominent merchant and postmaster. Mabel studied at Peace College (then Peace Institute) from 1907 to 1913. She also studied at Columbia University in New York and the Pennsylvania Academy of Fine Arts. Pugh gained notoriety for her block prints while working in New York City in the 1920s, then returned to North Carolina and taught at Peace College for 22 years. (Courtesy of Peace College.)

LITTLE CAROLINA BLUEBONNET

WRITTEN AND PICTURED BY MABEL PUGH

Mabel Pugh became Morrisville's first female author when she wrote and illustrated *Little Carolina Bluebonnet* in 1933. Set in the fictional village of Crabtree, Pugh's story reflects her life growing up in Morrisville. (Photograph by the author.)

Another remarkable Morrisville woman was Vallie Page Green, a missionary to Canton, China, for 43 years. Her efforts to spread Christianity there began in 1891 and ended in 1934, when she was forced to leave because of the advancing Japanese. (Courtesy of First Baptist Church of Morrisville.)

56

By 1935, the tobacco industry fueled the economies of Wake and surrounding counties. For Morrisville farmers, the rugged plant was a primary source of income. Pictured here are George and Irene Barbee Smith in a field of tobacco. (Courtesy of Dean Council.)

Another lucrative endeavor for some was moonshining. Both black and white Morrisvillians produced homemade liquor, which caused some locals to joke that the best way to ascertain that someone was from Morrisville was to observe the dent on his nose caused by drinking liquor out of Mason jars. (Courtesy of Faye Francisco.)

Adding to the town's reputation for liquor consumption was the opening of a new store by the Wake County Alcoholic Beverage Control Board. The store became one of the most popular stops, especially during football games. Revenues from the sales of spirits provided a generous portion of the town's $26,000 budget for 1947–1948. The town collected $1,000 from the "whiskey store" and another $3,232 from tax on the sale of wine and beer. (Photograph by the author.)

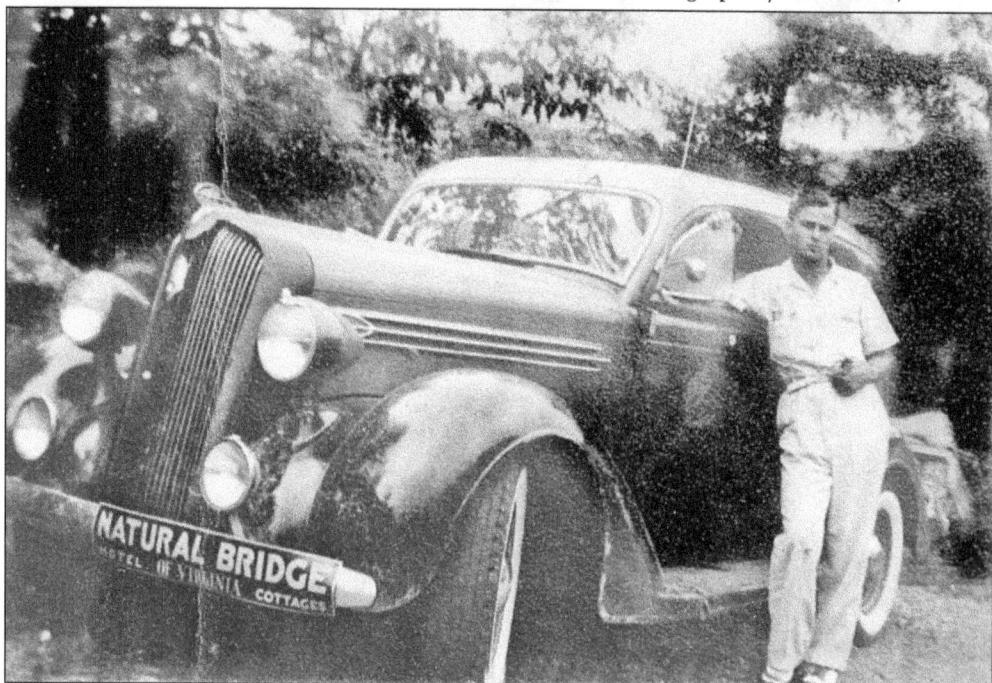

Clellan C. Nutt poses with his Pontiac, adorned with a bumper sticker for the popular tourist attraction in Virginia, Natural Bridge. (Courtesy of Betty Cotten Hardee.)

58

English-born photographer Albert Barden visited Morrisville and captured the town's mailman, Walter Churchill, standing beside the railroad tracks with Lettie and Eunice Bullock (left) and friend looking on. This area was the scene of two grisly train wrecks in 1933 and 1934 that destroyed several buildings and left an unknown number dead. (Courtesy of North Carolina Office of Archives and History.)

A 1938 aerial photograph reveals Morrisville's rural location in a patchwork of fields and forests. (Courtesy of North Carolina Office of Archives and History.)

Exie Cotten and his mother, Arletta, stand in front of their store on North Carolina Highway 54. Daughter Frances (left) and son Buck also pose with cousin Esmond Cotten. (Courtesy of Faye Francisco.)

Julia Cotten, just in the picture on the far right, ran the store, while her husband operated the adjoining garage. She sold beverages, snacks, and ice cream, making it a popular hangout for Morrisville teenagers. Jessie Lee Stutts (left), Emma Green (center), and Lilly Pitts are pictured visiting the store on a Sunday afternoon. (Courtesy of Emma Walton.)

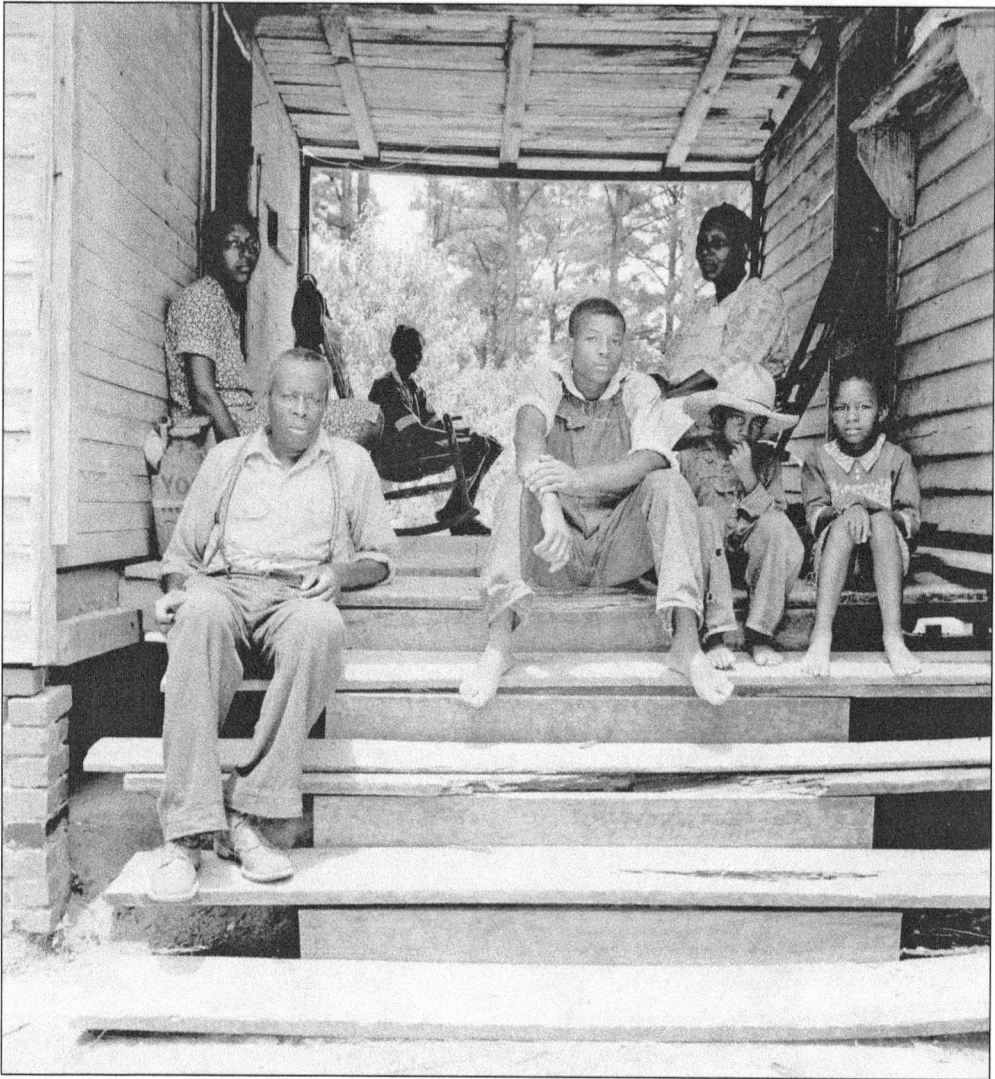

In July 1939, photographer Dorothea Lange spent a hot afternoon with farmer Zollie Lyons and his family. Lange, one of several photographers commissioned by the Farm Security Administration of the federal government to document the Great Depression, photographed the Lyons family on their farm southwest of Morrisville in the Upchurch community. Lange was widely acclaimed for capturing one of the most enduring images of the Depression, "Migrant Mother." (Courtesy of Library of Congress.)

Gene Autry and Johnny Mack Brown "visited" Morrisville in the form of Westerns shown on an outdoor screen. Merchant Bill Jones built the screen and showed free films next to the Ellis boardinghouse, making his profit on the sale of popcorn and drinks. (Courtesy Morrisville Town Archives.)

The bus accident that killed Patsy Long Neuman shocked Morrisville in 1941. The school bus she was riding struck a tree, but investigators determined that a mechanical failure rather than the inexperience of teenage driver Cecil Sears caused the wreck. (Courtesy of Tommy Tew.)

In World War II, as in all previous American conflicts, Morrisville men volunteered to fight. Army master sergeant Wilbur Sprite Barbee served with the 2nd Division from Africa to Italy, winning a remarkable eight Bronze Stars. (Dean Council.)

Howard J. Wimberly enlisted and rose to the rank of master sergeant in the U.S. Army. (Betty Cotten Hardee.)

Navy ensign Joe Reitano, far left, poses with his new wife's family, the Cottens, in 1942. (Courtesy of Betty Cotten Hardee.)

This image offers a glimpse of life on the home front in Morrisville during World War II. Clarence Yates was exempt from the draft because of his duties as deputy sheriff in Morrisville. With him are Nancy, Graham, and newborn son Robert. (Courtesy of Bob Yates.)

Faye Francisco (left) and a friend visiting from Raleigh, Joanne Powell, play with toys in front of the Franciscos' log cabin. Faye's father, Laddie Franciso, came from Virginia to help build Duke University. With the arrival of war, Laddie worked to help build Fort Bragg in Fayetteville. Each weekend, he would return home with new toys for Faye and scrap materials to enlarge their small home. (Courtesy of Faye Francisco Godbold.)

Siblings Nancy and Clayborn Council pose together on a fall afternoon in 1943. Their mother sent this photograph to a farm magazine, which published it and awarded her a prize of $5. (Courtesy of Dean Council.)

Gov. Melville Broughton and daughter Alice christen the *Raleigh Flyer*. The plane was part of Eastern Airlines' inaugural round-trip service between the Triangle area and Washington, D.C., in 1942. (North Carolina Office of Archives and History.)

On May 1, 1943, Eastern Airlines landed the first airplane at one of the three newly completed landing strips at the Raleigh-Durham Air Field outside Morrisville. When the airfield was taken over by the federal government during World War II, Eastern Airlines was permitted use of the field for limited service to New York and Miami. Flights north stopped in Richmond, Washington, Baltimore, and Philadelphia during the four-hour trip to New York. Flights south stopped in Charleston, Savannah, Jacksonville, Orlando, Vero Beach, and West Palm during the six-hour trip to Miami. (Courtesy of North Carolina Office of Archives and History.)

Mabel Pugh made this charcoal study of eight-year-old Betty Cotten in 1943 for a painting called *Little Brown Betty.* Betty remembered that she had to pose all summer, and the constant wear, washing, and starching of the dress caused it to eventually fall apart. (Courtesy of Betty Cotten Hardee.)

Life returned to normal after World War II, as evidenced by this Barbee family reunion in 1946. Ida Barbee, in a polka-dot dress, stands with her seven children (from left to right and youngest to oldest), Alberta "Teddy" Barbee Council, Margaret Barbee Holt, Tom Barbee, Wilbur Barbee, Wallace Barbee, Evelyn Barbee Smaw, and Irene Barbee Smith. (Courtesy of Dean Council.)

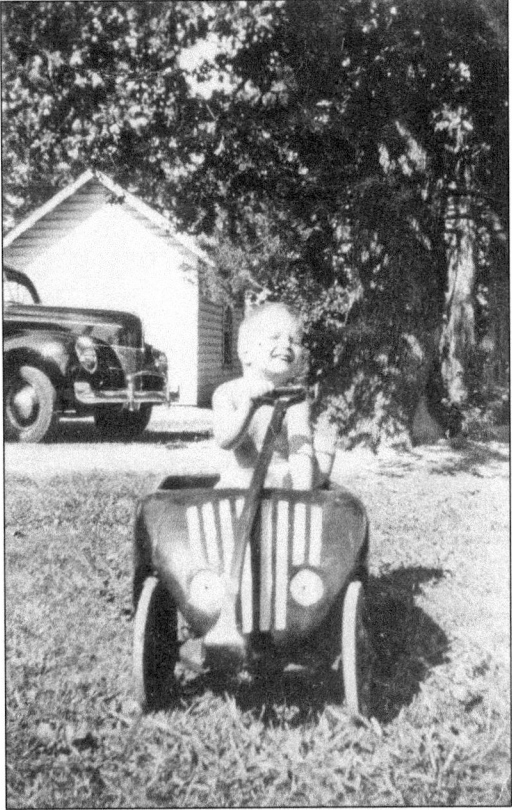

An excited Robert Yates enjoys his wagon and reflects the joy the town experienced after World War II ended. (Courtesy of Bob Yates.)

George Smith poses proudly in front of slaughtered hogs on a cool day in 1945. (Courtesy of Dean Council.)

In 1946, Forehand's Store was located on the road between Morrisville and Durham. Ruth Couch remembered that her brother Floyd looked forward to walking to the store to buy 5¢ bottles of coke and Mary Jane candies with his beagle, Rover. He would share the candy with Rover on the journey home. (Courtesy of Johnnie Evans.)

Faye Francisco and her mother enjoy an afternoon in the snow in the late 1940s. McLawHorn Café on North Carolina Highway 54 is visible in the background. (Courtesy of Faye Francisco Godbold.)

In the days of segregated libraries, this bookmobile traveled throughout Wake County and stopped in communities like Shiloh, offering books to local residents. This image, taken in 1946, shows visitors arriving on foot and by wagon to borrow books. (Courtesy of Richard B. Harrison Library.)

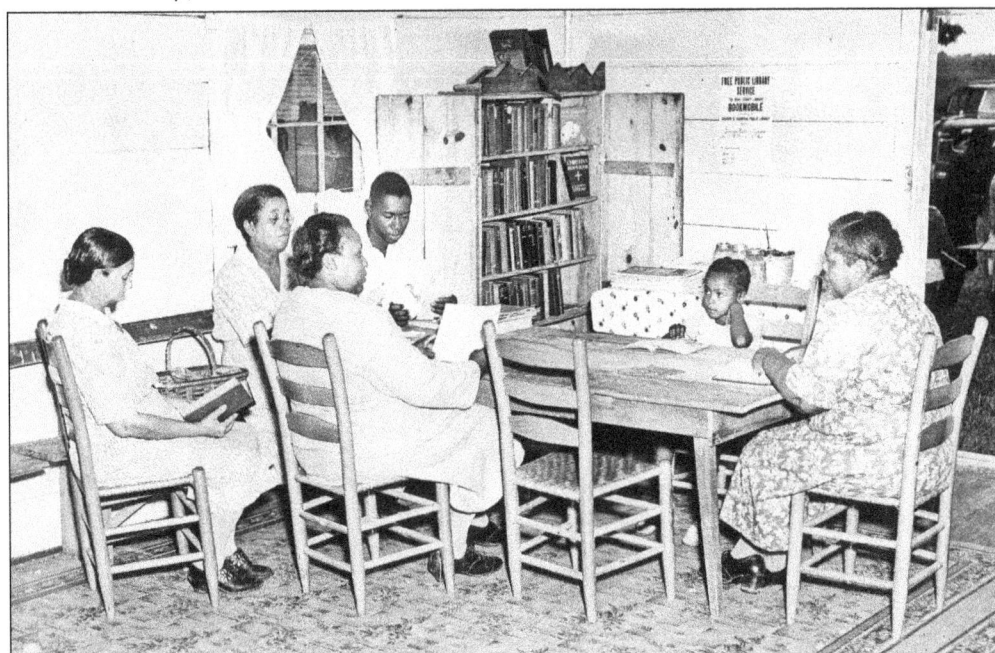

Once a month, the bookmobile visited the Shiloh Baptist Church, allowing local residents to borrow and return books. These rural book exchanges were sponsored by the Richard B. Harrison Library in Raleigh, founded by Mollie Huston Lee, the first African American librarian in Wake County. (Courtesy of Richard B. Harrison Library.)

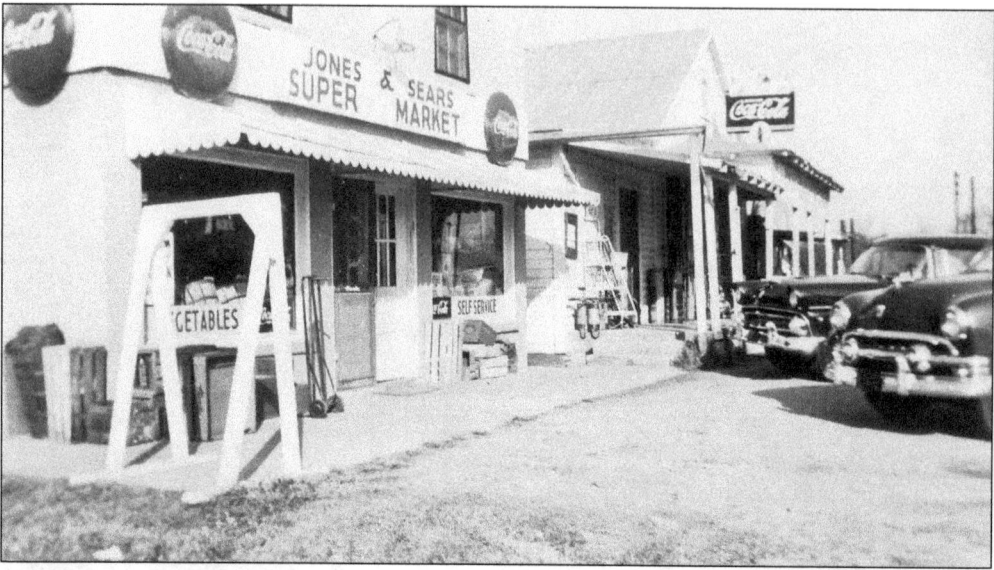

William Dodd's store was destroyed in the town's last major train wreck in 1934. Sometime afterwards, he rebuilt his store, and, by 1941, he had sold it to Bill Jones. Jones took on Cecil Sears as a partner, and the two operated a grocery and hardware store out of the building. (Courtesy of Morrisville Town Archives.)

Bill Jones and Cecil Sears (left) provided Morrisville with its only grocery store in 1942. (Courtesy of Morrisville Town Archives.)

Lee Jones strikes a pose on the porch of the Jones and Sears Grocery. (Courtesy of Edythe Smith Yates.)

A group of cousins passes the time on a hot summer afternoon. From left to right are Louise Smaw, Nancy Council, Martha Kay Barbee, Gene Barbee, and Clayborn Council. (Courtesy of Dean Council.)

Irene Barbee Smith has some fun with her nephew, Clayborn Council, in 1953. (Courtesy of Dean Council.)

Young Frank Holden pushes a plow in 1948, recreating a common sight seen while passing through the surrounding countryside during that era. (Courtesy of Dean Council.)

Several members of the Morrisville Baptist Church pose in the parking lot on a Sunday afternoon. From left to right are Bill White, Franklin Upchurch, Floyd Mulholland, Dallas Marshburn, Carl Light, Kader Upchurch, John Medlin, Rev. Norman Mitchell, and B. C. Olive. The Weston Edwards home stands in the background. (Courtesy of First Baptist Church of Morrisville.)

To capitalize on the increased automobile traffic on North Carolina Highway 54 after World War II, Exie Cotten Sr. erected these two buildings. The smaller building was constructed in the early 1950s to house Morrisville's ever-popular liquor store, and the larger structure, a café, was built 10 years later. (Photograph by the author.)

For decades, this device helped Morrisvillians communicate with the rest of the world. Mail pouches hung from this pole were snatched by passing trains. (Courtesy of Betty King Nordan.)

Four

AWAKING FROM
A DEEP SLEEP
1950–2007

A few festive souls dress up in their funniest clothes for a Tacky Party after Bible class in 1950. From left to right are Luther Barbee, Ida Barbee, Irene Barbee Smith, Annie Nutt, Narvie Maynard, Mr. and Mrs. Mann, and Mr. and Mrs. E. K. Carroll. (Courtesy of Dean Council.)

Margaret Jane Green and her husband traveled to Durham and sat in the studio of photographer William "Willie" Thomas Jones. Durham, like Raleigh, had a growing number of black professionals, and Jones was one of them. He opened his studio there in 1930. (Courtesy of Morrisville Town Archives.)

Seeming to mirror Tobacco Road basketball rivalries, Irene Barbee Smith (left) and Alberta Barbee Council contest possession of the ball while grandmother Ida Barbee waits to receive a pass. (Courtesy of Dean Council.)

Milton Holt (left) and Bruce Council became brothers-in-law after they married the Barbee sisters, Margaret and Alberta. (Courtesy of Dean Council.)

The possibility of landing construction contracts at the airport drew Johnnie Robertson to Morrisville. He operated a construction business and worked on several municipal projects in town. He also became the town's longest-serving mayor. (Courtesy Morrisville Town Archives.)

The Cotten sisters, (seated, left to right) Dorothy, Dixie, Celestine, and Betty (standing in the back), celebrate Dorothy's 26th birthday in August 1954. (Courtesy of Betty Cotten Hardee.)

Ethel (right) and Irene Clements pose for this touching portrait in Raleigh in the 1960s. Both sisters developed a love of music and were educated at Elon College. Ethel taught music at the local Green Hope School, and she married a former member of the army band. (Courtesy of Emma Walton.)

Morrisville children were warned to stay away from the area around a certain service station. Besides selling liquor to anyone who could put money on the counter, there were several cabins to the rear of the store often used by prostitutes. (Courtesy of Faye Francisco.)

Jones and Sears remodeled their joint stores and reopened as a Red and White supermarket. (Courtesy of Morrisville Town Archives.)

Fire chief Cecil Sears (far left) poses with members of the Morrisville Fire Department: (left to right) Tommy Tew, Jim Best, Bob Holsclaw, Paul "Bo" Walton, and Raymon Broadwell. (Courtesy of Tommy Tew.)

In August 1955, Morrisville purchased a Korean War surplus oil truck to use as the town fire engine. This picture shows the 2.5-ton truck before it was converted. (Courtesy of Carl V. Light.)

Out for an afternoon of summer fun are, from left to right, Barbara Hansley Perry, Edith Smith Yates, and Jean Forbes Rogers. (Courtesy of Bob Yates.)

In 1953, Barbara Hansley Perry was crowned Cary High School's football queen. (Courtesy of Edythe Smith Yates.)

The talented dog Butch demonstrates his skill with help from assistant Robert Yates. In the background stand both the home and store built by Charles Maynard. (Courtesy of Bob Yates.)

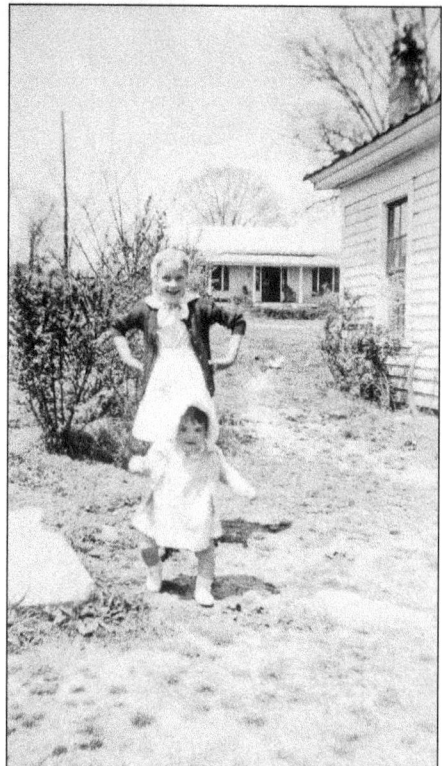

Bessie Olive and young friend Linda Knight (foreground) play in the yard. (Courtesy of Betty King Nordan.)

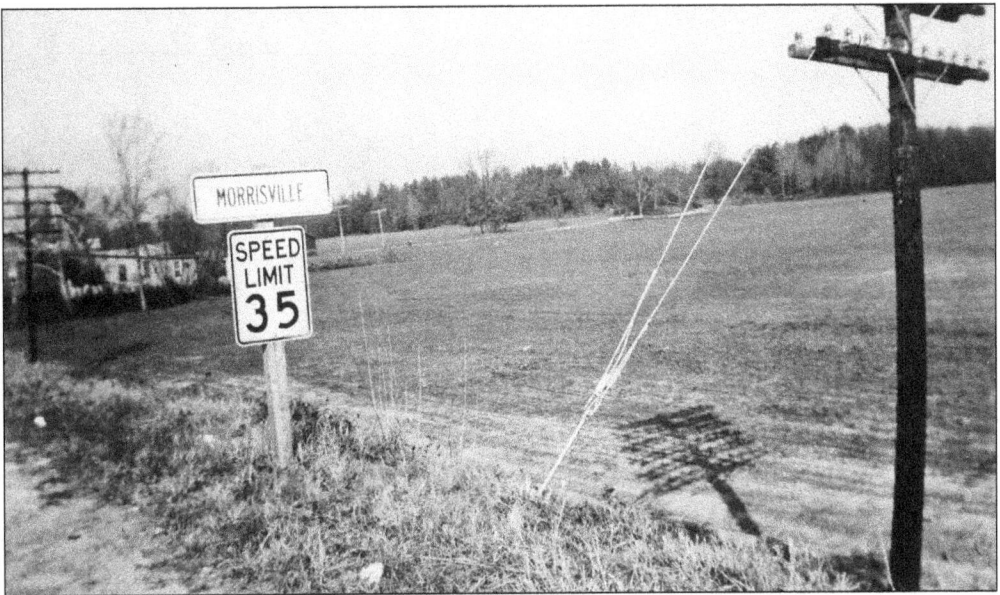

Visitors entering Morrisville from Raleigh were greeted by this sign. The town had actually been unincorporated in 1933. It was not until 1947 that it was it was once again officially recognized as a town. (Courtesy Morrisville Town Archives.)

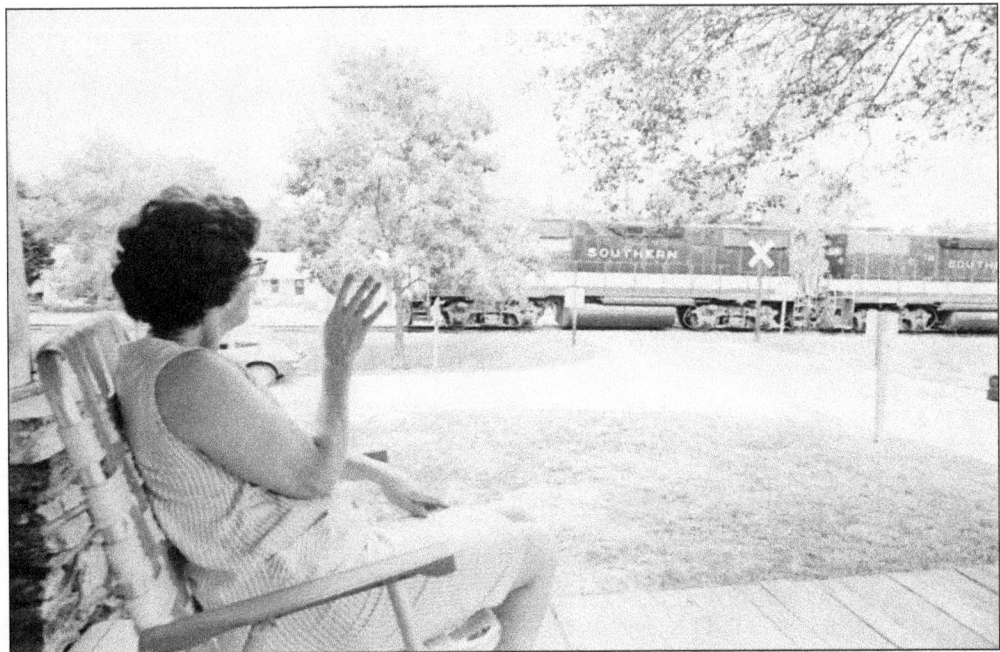

The train was a part of daily life in Morrisville, but in the early 1950s, passenger service ended, leaving residents to wave at passing cars rather than boarding them. (Courtesy of *News and Observer* and North Carolina Office of Archives and History.)

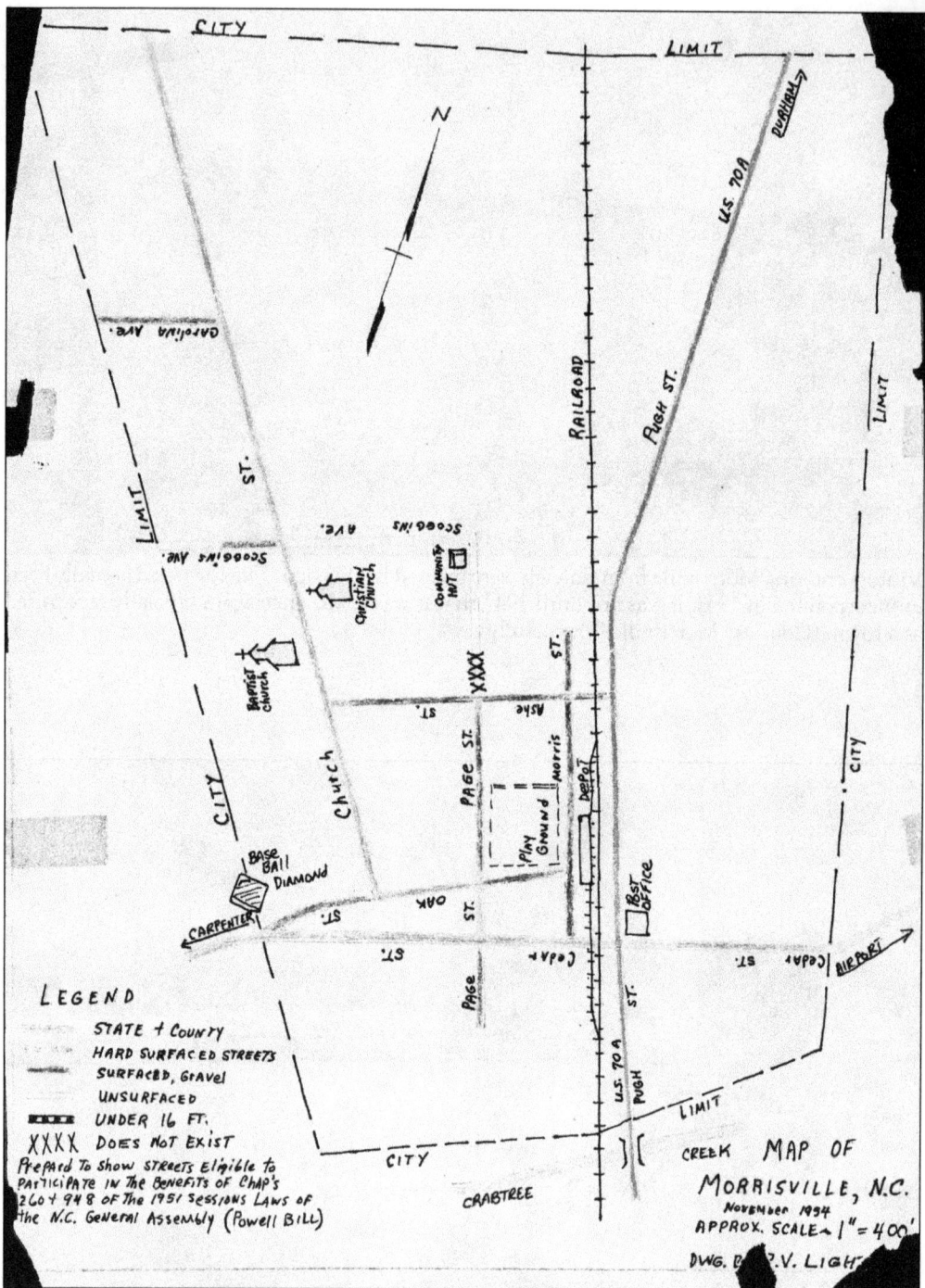

This map was drawn in 1951 to show the town's eligibility to receive capital-improvement funds provided by the Powell Bill. This legislation, advocated by the State Municipal Road Commission and "roads governor" W. Kerr Scott, urged the state government to increase funding to improve streets in cities and towns across the state. (Courtesy of Morrisville Town Archives.)

This view looking south along the old mill lot is typical of many of the town's streets that were unpaved and unnamed. (Courtesy of Morrisville Town Archives.)

Money from passage of the Powell Bill transformed Morrisville's landscape. Local residents watch as dusty Page Street is paved. (Courtesy of Morrisville Town Archives.)

Ash Street was also paved during this time. Initially one of two streets that made a grade crossing of the railroad, it joined North Carolina Highway 54 in front of Strickland's gas station. (Courtesy of Morrisville Town Archives.)

The Morrisville Baptist Church also underwent a period of growth in the early 1950s under the leadership of Rev. Cecil Watson. Plans were drawn up for a 2-story, 16-room wing that would house a library, pastor's study, baptistery, kitchen, and dining room. Reverend Watson led the ground-breaking ceremony in May 1954. (Courtesy of Carl V. Light.)

Work continued on the new wing throughout the summer and was finally completed on the second Sunday in November 1954. (Courtesy of First Baptist Church of Morrisville.)

In October 1955, the Raleigh-Durham Airport opened a new building and expanded their service. (Courtesy of North Carolina Office of Archives and History.)

This airport expansion attracted pilots like Russian-born Igor Bensen, the world's leading exponent of the lightweight, home-built rotorcraft. In this photograph, he demonstrates his B-10 Prop-Copter VTOL aircraft prototype on August 6, 1958. Bensen formed the Bensen Aircraft Corporation in 1953, offering a range of do-it-yourself helicopters and autogiros. The B-10 was powered by two 72-horsepower McCulloch engines, each driving a horizontal propeller. (Courtesy of North Carolina Office of Archives and History.)

The influence of contemporary architecture is seen in this home constructed by Johnny Robertson in 1954. The front exterior chimney makes it a unique structure in Morrisville. (Courtesy of Morrisville Town Archives.)

On the heels of Powell Bill improvements, Carolina Power and Light Company sponsored the Finer Carolina contest, which gave out additional money for community improvements. Several major projects took place in town, such as naming and marking Morrisville's streets, cleaning up vacant lots, and repainting some of the town's 55 homes. (Courtesy of Morrisville Town Archives.)

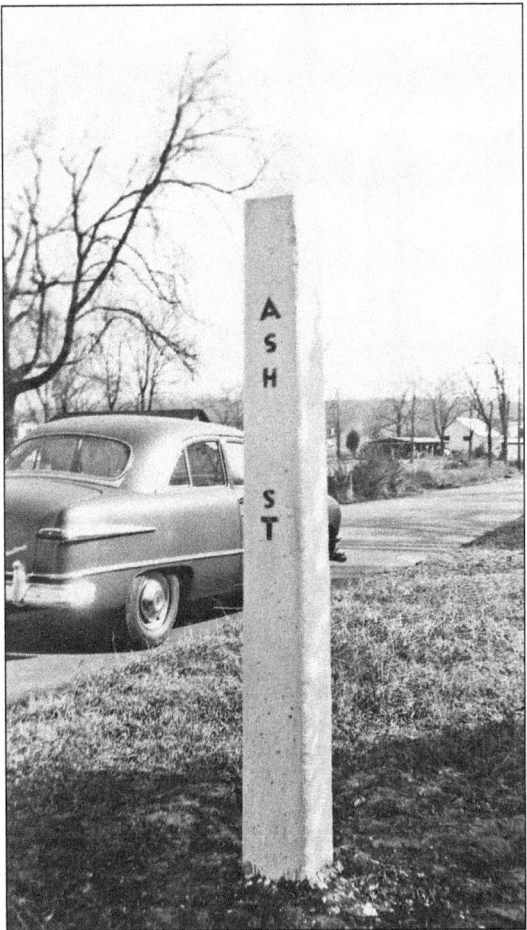

A significant project at this time was the construction of a community center. A lot was selected and deeded to the town for free. The future Scoggins Avenue was graded to provide access to the new facility. (Courtesy of Morrisville Town Archives.)

With absolutely no money to fund the $1,400 project, volunteers stepped forward to begin work on the building. (Courtesy of Morrisville Town Archives.)

To help pay for the project, Morrisville residents sponsored several fund-raising programs, such as a "hillbilly show" and a carnival. By May 1957, enough money had been raised to complete construction of the center's walls. (Courtesy of Carl V. Light.)

As part of the town's participation in the Finer Carolina competition, residents worked on another project that filled an important need in their community. A new 3-acre baseball field was built on the town's western border, and a team organized. Additionally, a playground and other sports areas were organized in the former knitting mill lot along Page Street. (Courtesy of Morrisville Town Archives.)

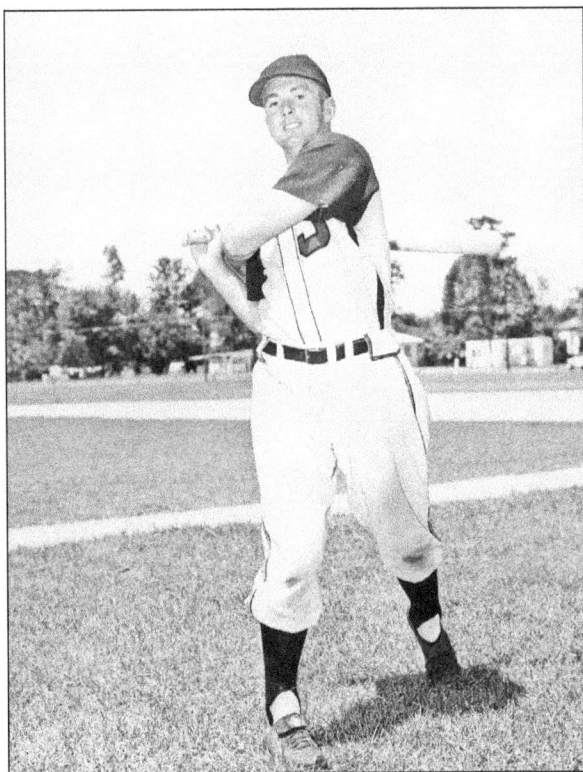

Clayborn Council was the catcher for the 1957 Selma Giants, which played in the Alabama-Florida League, a Class D minor league of teams mostly in the Deep South. (Courtesy of Dean Council.)

Photographs of Pres. Dwight D. Eisenhower and North Carolina governor Luther Hodges grace the dedication ceremony for Morrisville's new post office. Among those seated on the flatbed truck stage are town commissioners E. K. Carroll, Olive Terrell, Evelyn Hansley, Helen Johnson, Sue Johnson, and Mayor Johnny Robertson and wife, Francis. (Courtesy of Barbara Hansley Perry.)

The dedication for the new town post office took place adjacent to the now-destroyed Perry house at the corner of North Carolina Highway 54 and Aviation Parkway. Residents and weary members of the band enjoy the day's activities. (Courtesy of Barbara Hansley Perry.)

Mayor Johnny Robertson and his wife, Frances (right), chat with the town's postmistress, Helen Johnson, at the dedication of Morrisville's new post office. (Courtesy of Evelyn Hansley.)

The creation of the Research Triangle Park in 1958 would drastically alter Morrisville in the coming decades. The Hanes Building was the first constructed in the new park and served as it headquarters for a number of years. It is now part of the Research Triangle Institute campus. (Courtesy of Olivia Raney Library.)

In 1960, the Morrisville Baptist Church built a new a parsonage on the site of the church's original parsonage. (Courtesy of Morrisville Town Archives.)

A late snow in April 1960 paralyzed daily life in Morrisville. (Courtesy of Carl V. Light.)

Flanked by a shoeshine chair and bottles of hair tonic, Tommy Tew stands in his barbershop, which first opened in 1960. Tew's shop was located on North Carolina Highway 54 until 1979, when he built a new shop behind his home on Aviation Parkway. In 2007, Tew celebrated his 47th year cutting hair in Morrisville. (Courtesy of North Carolina Office of Archives and History.)

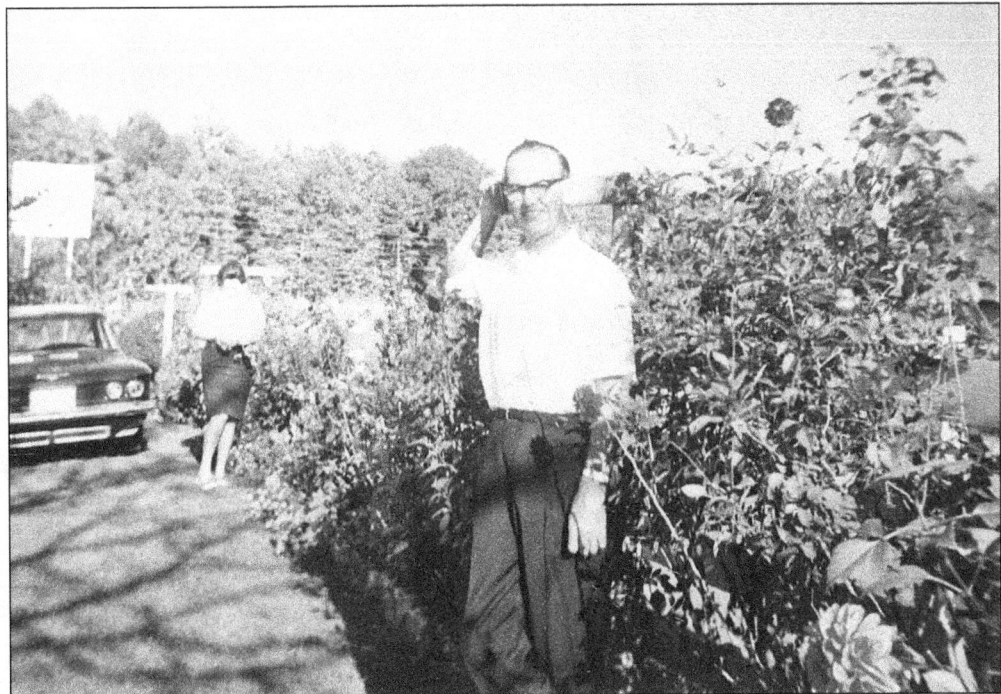

Overcoming the limits of Morrisville's notoriously poor soil, Carl Light stands proudly next to his flourishing rose garden. (Courtesy of Carl V. Light.)

A corn crop is destroyed when summer rains cause Crabtree Creek to wash over its banks. (Courtesy of Faye Francisco.)

The Baptists were the first religious group to establish a church in Wake County, which they did as early as 1761. New Lights broke away from the New England Congregationalists in Connecticut, moved southward into present Randolph County in the 1750s, and helped to establish New Light Church in northwestern Wake about 1775. Baptists have always been the most popular sect in the county because of their emphasis on congregational autonomy. The original Morrisville Baptist Church was built with two separate entrance doors, a remnant of bygone customs when men and women were separated in their congregations. (Courtesy of First Baptist Church of Morrisville.)

Eugene Light and Veronica Mulholland are crowned May Day King and Queen in 1963. (Courtesy of the First Baptist Church of Morrisville.)

In May 1963, this coronation was held at the Morrisville Baptist Church. (Courtesy of First Morrisville Baptist Church.)

Children play on the front steps of the Morrisville Baptist Church after Sunday school in June 1963. (Courtesy of First Baptist Church of Morrisville.)

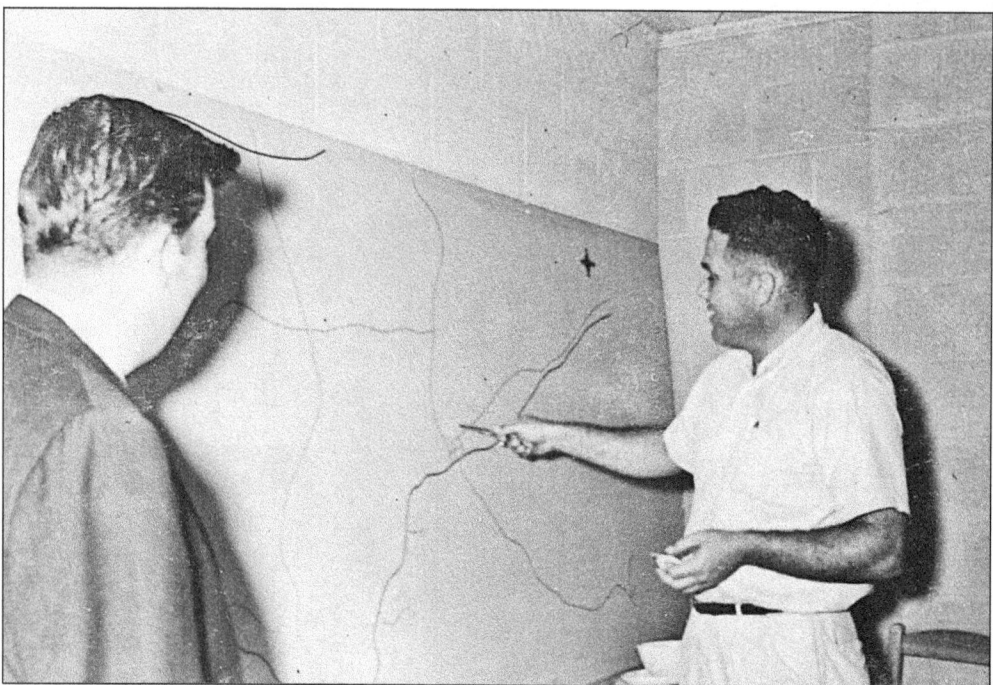

Two members of the First Baptist Church of Morrisville divide up the community in preparation for dispatching missionaries. (Courtesy of First Baptist Church of Morrisville.)

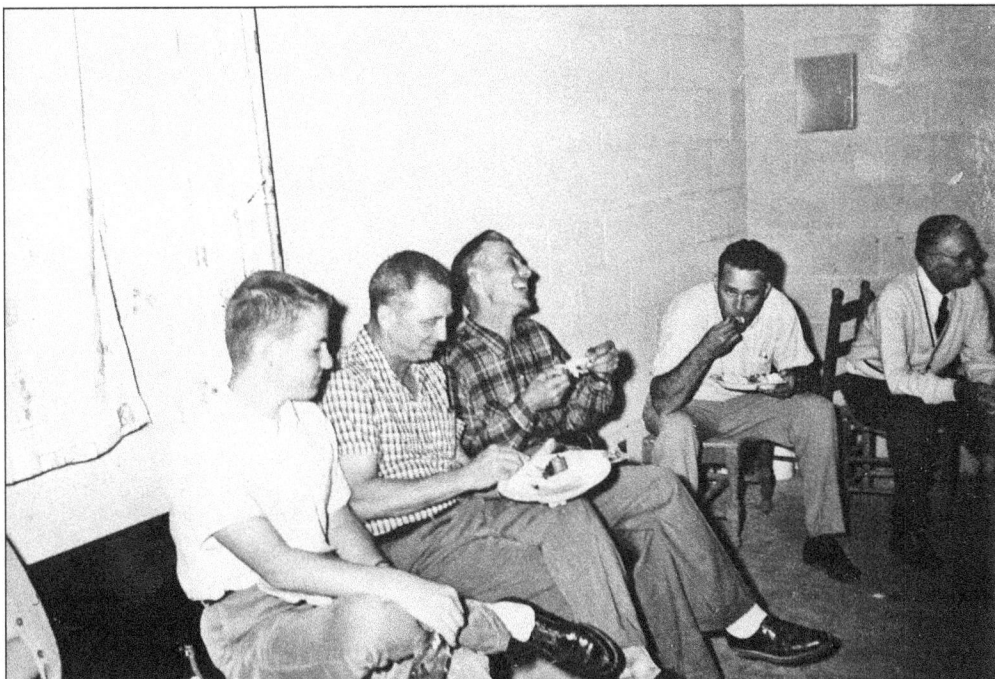

A group of young men enjoy a joke during a barbecue sponsored by Morrisville Baptist Church in May 1963. (Courtesy of First Baptist Church of Morrisville.)

Triplets Allison (left), Angie (center), and Anita Cotten were born on Christmas Day, 1964. (Courtesy of Emma Walton.)

Little by little, the Morrisville Fire Department expanded its fleet of trucks. A glimpse of the early fire department can be seen on the left. (Courtesy of the Town of Morrisville.)

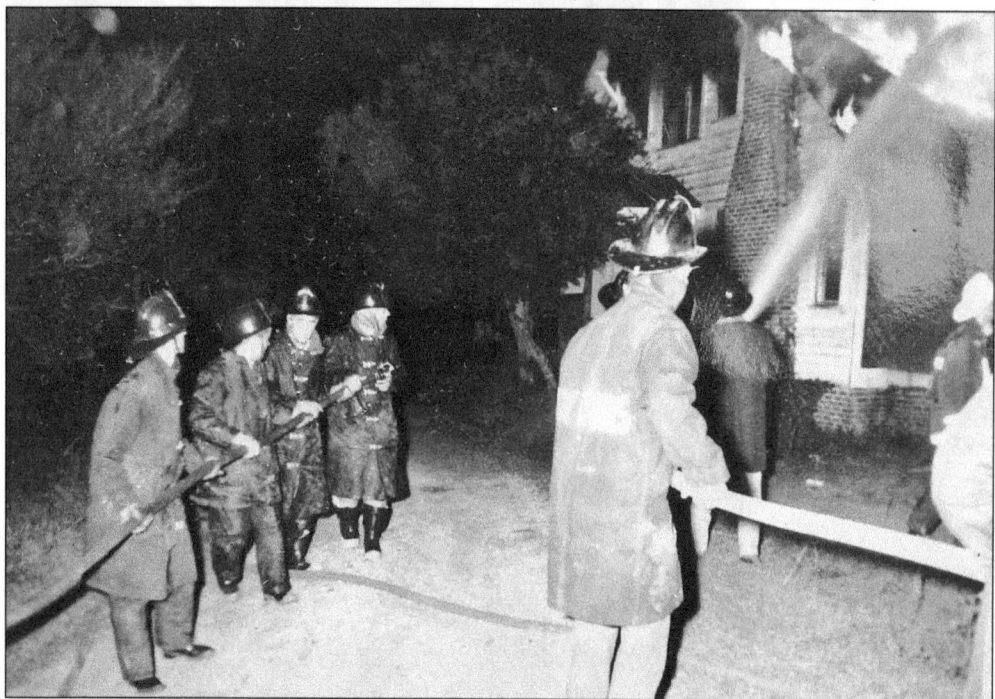

The men of the Morrisville Fire Department are pictured in action battling a house fire. (Courtesy of First Baptist Church of Morrisville.)

Firefighters and their families are hard at work during a fund-raiser dinner held at the Morrisville Fire Department. The map on the wall shows the district the early department covered. (Courtesy of First Baptist Church of Morrisville.)

The Green Hope School, built in 1927, hosted grades 1 through 12 until 1952, when it was renamed Green Hope Elementary School. It was the first accredited rural school in Wake County and, by 1963, it served 172 students, all of them white. On August 15, 1963, at 1:00 a.m., the building caught fire, and despite the response by local fire departments, the school was destroyed. The cause of fire was officially described as "suspicious circumstances," and opposition to racial integration of the local schools was suspected to be the motive. (Courtesy of Morrisville Town Archives.)

By 1928, Morrisville's African American community had started a church along the railroad tracks on Morris Street. But antagonism from the white community intimidated several of the church's ministers and kept the congregation small. Eventually land was given for a new church on the town's western outskirts, and in July 1951 the church held its first official ceremony in the newly reamed Hatcher's Grove Baptist Church. This image, taken in 1970, shows Rev. Robert L. Fuller standing with church members in front of the original church building. (Courtesy of Lillie Jones.)

Until the 1980s, Morrisville still retained much of its rural character. (Courtesy of North Carolina Office of Archives and History.)

A wide-angle lens distorts the railroad tracks through Morrisville but captures the heart of the town as it appeared in the late 1970s. Two landmarks visible in this picture have disappeared: the original sidetrack on the right and the Perry gas station on the left. (Courtesy of North Carolina Office of Archives and History.)

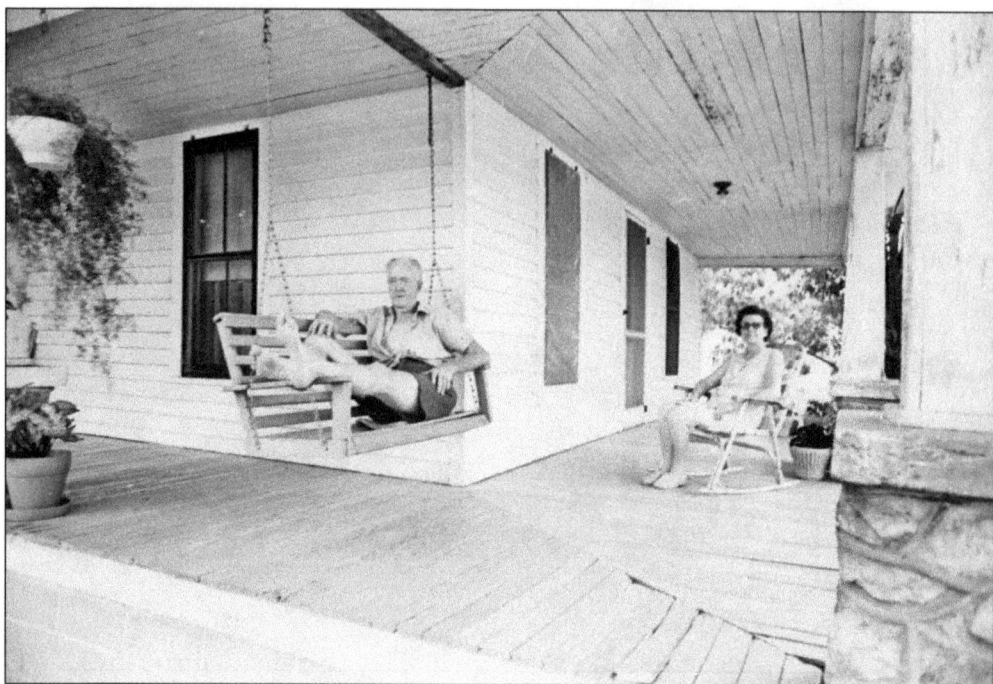

Marguerite and Howard Davis relax on a summer day, seated on the porch of the William Penny house on Morris Street. (Courtesy of North Carolina Office of Archives and History.)

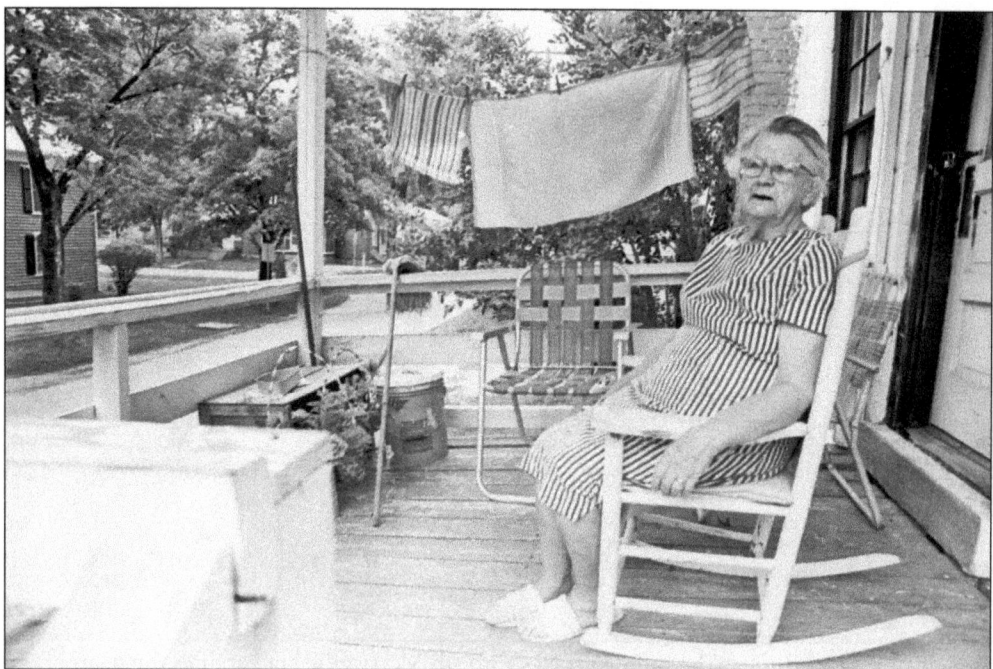

Sitting on the porch of her apartment above the Red and White grocery store, Fannie Upchurch Sears surveys Morrisville's tree-lined lots in the summer of 1977. (Courtesy of North Carolina Office of Archives and History.)

On July 14, 1976, the congregation of the Morrisville Christian Church disbanded after a disagreement with its minister. Afterwards the church building was sold to the town of Morrisville, and it housed first the town hall and later the chamber of commerce. (Courtesy of Morrisville Town Archives.)

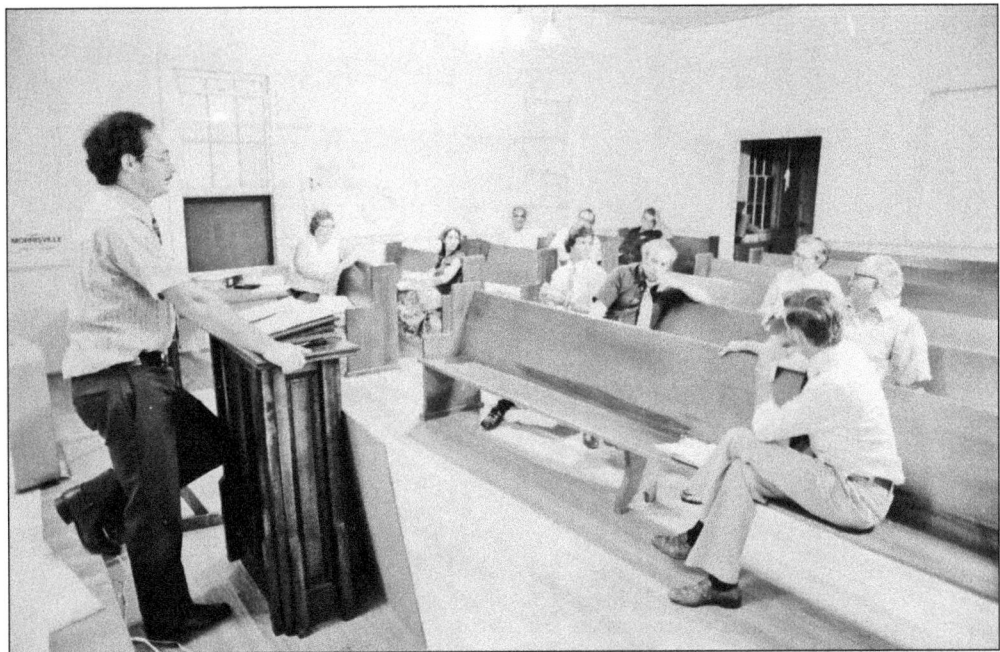

Wade Davis led this typical town hall meeting in 1977 in the former sanctuary of the disbanded Christian church. (Courtesy of North Carolina Office of Archives and History.)

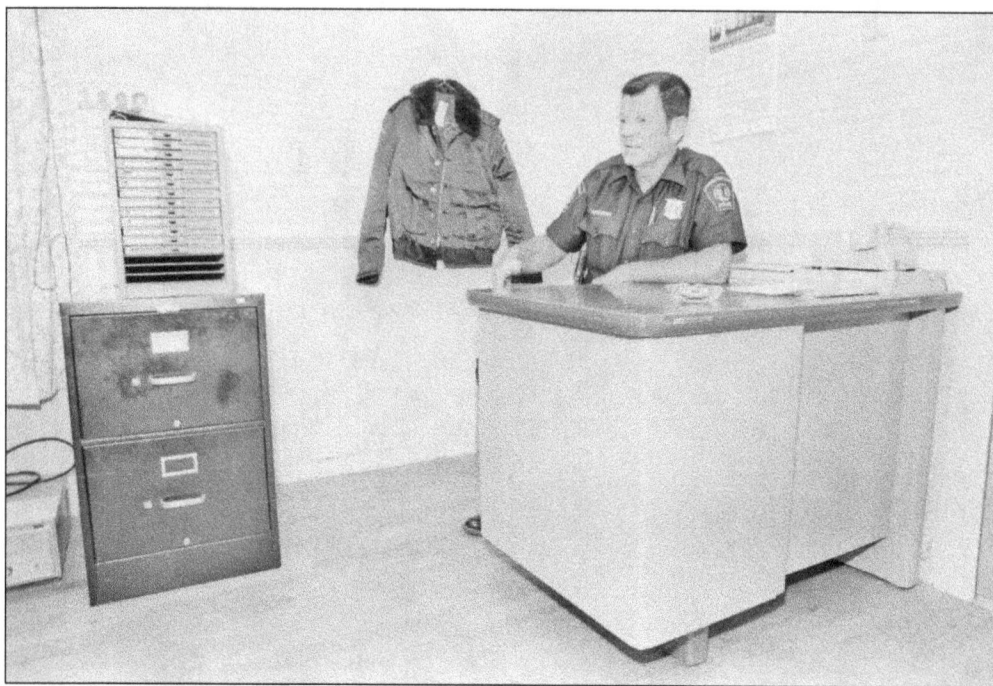

In 1977, the single officer of Morrisville's police department was Pat Craddock, seen here at his desk inside the town hall. (Courtesy of North Carolina Office of Archives and History.)

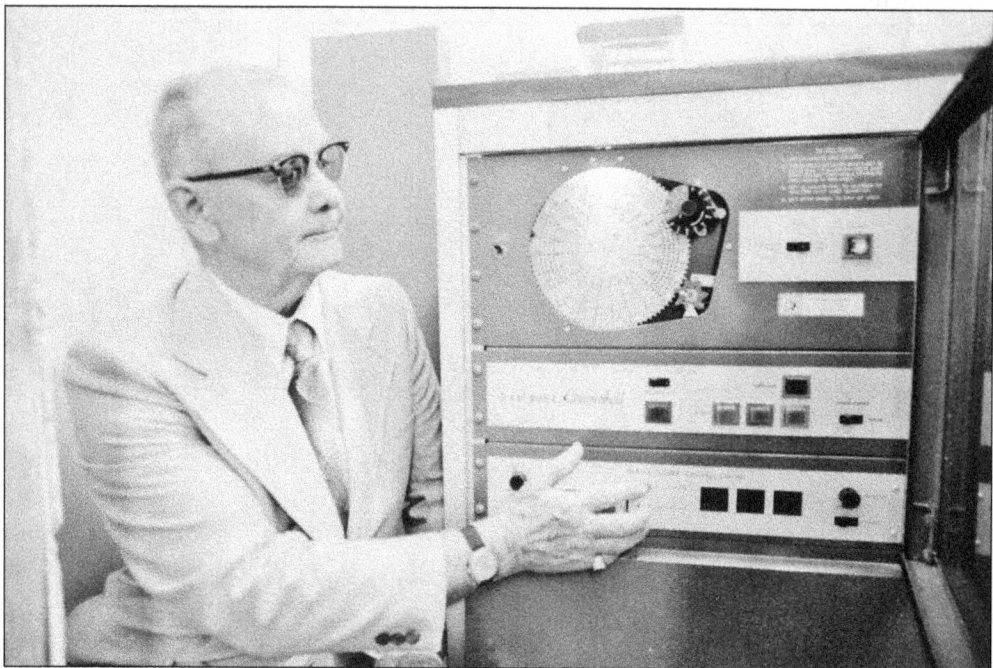

Aldridge Ferrall tests the new electronic chimes that replaced the bells at the First Baptist Church of Morrisville in 1977. (Courtesy of North Carolina Office of Archives and History.)

Entertainment for Morrisville's children consisted of playing in Crabtree Creek, throwing rocks, or daring each other to walk across the train trestle. Bicycles, even those with flat tires, gave youngsters an additional tool with which to enjoy summer afternoons. (Courtesy of North Carolina Office of Archives and History.)

Morrisville's rural housing in the mid-1970s was still dominated by 19th-century farmhouses. (Courtesy of North Carolina Division of Archives and History.)

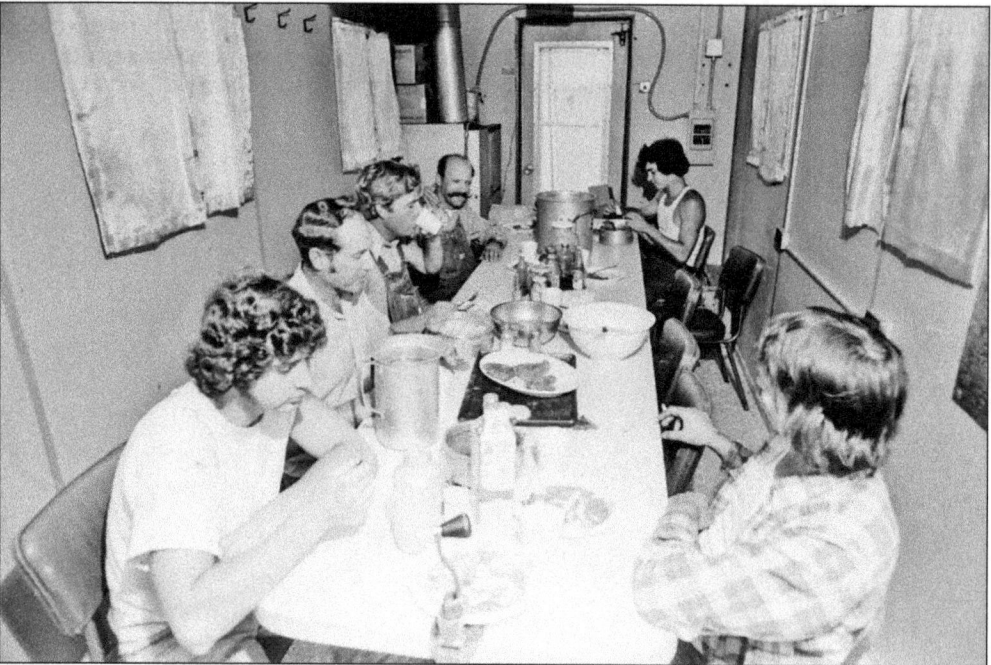

Railroad workers enjoy breakfast aboard a railcar in the summer of 1977. (Courtesy of North Carolina Office of Archives and History.)

Many who had left the rural setting of Morrisville and moved into the growing cities of Raleigh and Durham still had family in the country. E. P. Oats traveled back to pick beans in his daughter's garden on a hot August afternoon. (Courtesy of North Carolina Office of Archives and History.)

By the 1980s, Morrisville Police Department had grown to a force of seven officers and was headquartered in the former community hut. (Courtesy of Morrisville Town Archives.)

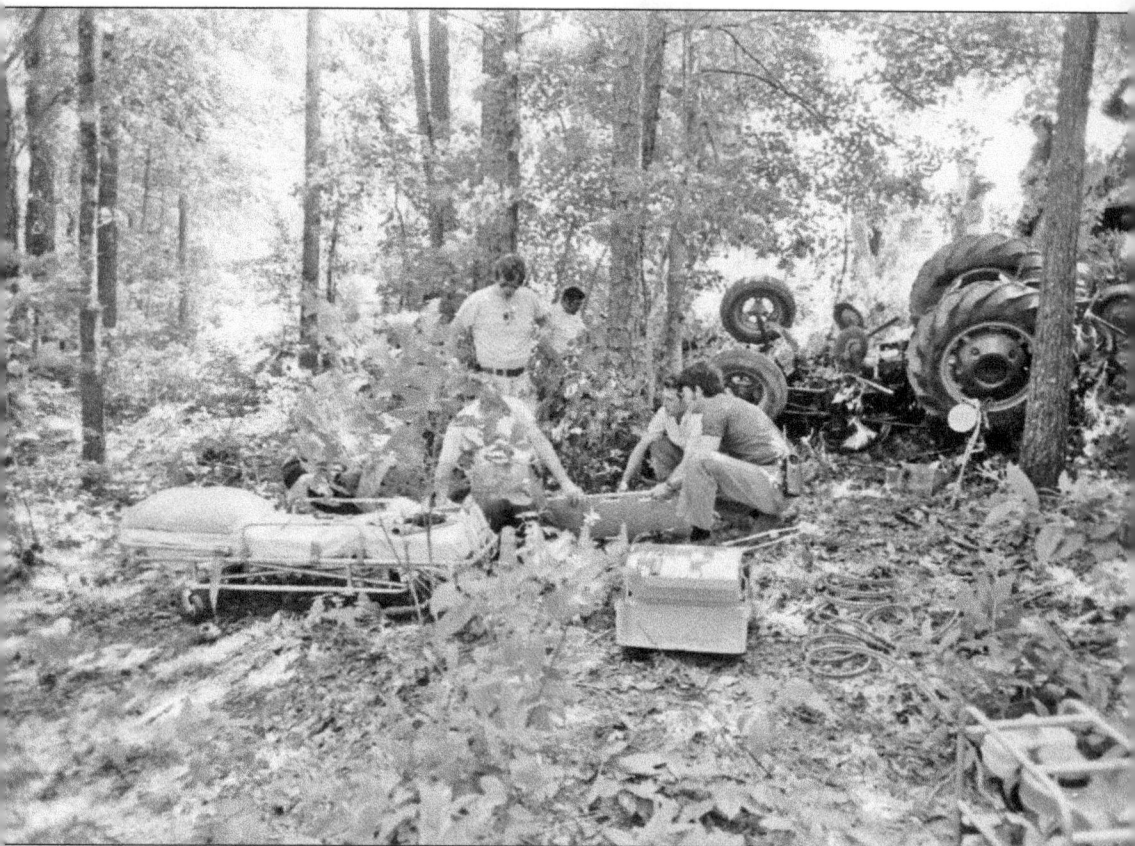

Silas Dampere was lucky to escape injury the first time he rolled his tractor on a Saturday in April 1977. After spending the day making repairs, Dampere resumed work in his field. He had plowed a single row when the tractor once again flipped, trapping him underneath the steering wheel. After three hours, rescue workers freed him from the wreck, but he died three days later of pneumonia. (Courtesy of North Carolina Office of Archives and History.)

The town of Morrisville began celebrating its history in festivals like this one in 1981. (Courtesy of North Carolina Office of Archives and History.)

Mrs. Joseph Bell holds a painting of her home, originally the homestead of the Maynard family, who arrived in the late 18th century. The Maynard house is thought to have been a stop for stagecoaches traveling between the state capital in Raleigh and the university in Chapel Hill. (Courtesy of Olivia Raney Library.)

Morrisville mayor Ernest Lumley swears in Floyd Enzor to serve out the term of Commissioner Johnny Johnson. (Courtesy of Morrisville Town Archives.)

The sounds of roaring go-carts could be heard for miles around the Morrisville Speedway. A racer prepares to hit the track in June 1983. (Courtesy of North Carolina Office of Archives and History.)

Ninety-six-year-old Julia (left) and her sister-in-law, Essie Leona Cotten, sit on the front porch on a summer afternoon. Many considered Essie to be Morrisville's Florence Nightingale, providing nursing to sick villagers. (Courtesy of Betty Cotten Hardee.)

Paul "Bo" Walton became the town's unofficial sanitation engineer in 1950. For the next 36 years he, with his dog Caesar, collected Morrisville's garbage. In 1986, Bo finally said good-bye to this faithful old truck. (Courtesy of Emma Walton.)

Inspired by a dream, the Sharma family decided to erect a Hindu temple. After they chose a site in Morrisville, friends asked why they were going to build in "the jungle." But the rural location didn't dissuade the Sharmas, and in December 1986, construction began on the main building. An activity hall was added in July 2000. (Photograph by the author.)

Beginning with only 25 members, Morrisville's Hindu temple has grown to become the largest in the eastern half of the state with over 2,000 members. (Photograph by the author.)

A new town hall was needed to cope with the explosion of growth in the early 1990s. From a platform adorned with architectural drawings, Mayor Ernest Lumley speaks at the ground-breaking ceremony for the new building in 1991. (Courtesy of Morrisville Town Archives.)

This new town hall was constructed on the site of the old baseball field. (Courtesy of Morrisville Town Archives.)

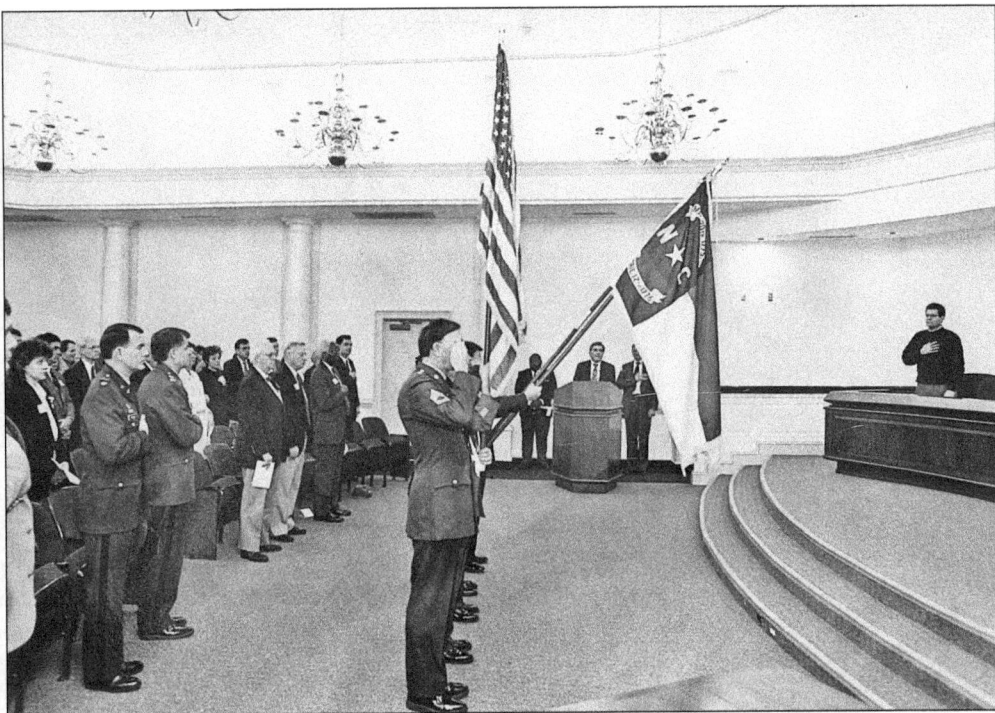

Soldiers from Morrisville's National Guard units form a color guard and lead the Pledge of Allegiance at the dedication of the new town hall on December 29, 1992. (Courtesy of Morrisville Town Archives.)

Capt. Ed Mauldin leads a group of reenactors in the early 1990s as they recreate the organization of the Cedar Fork Rifles at the Page House. (Courtesy of Mary Page Ferrell.)

In the early 1990s, the popularity of outlet centers grew, and it peaked with 329 across the United States in 1996. The first major shopping outlet for Morrisville was the Prime Outlet mall, built along the busy Interstate 40 and Airport Boulevard. (Courtesy of Morrisville Town Archives.)

Morrisville's Day in the Park celebration developed into the biggest event sponsored by the town. (Courtesy of Morrisville Town Archives.)

Margaret Broadwell became Morrisville's first female mayor in 1995 after taking over the office from Ernest Lumley. (Courtesy of Morrisville Town Archives.)

Participants line up in formation for Morrisville's first Christmas parade in 1996. (Courtesy of Morrisville Town Archives.)

The Greens are among the most prolific families of Morrisville. Here they gather for the 60th birthday of sister Emma, known as "Tet." From left to right are Jack, Ruth, William, Lesbia, Frank, Elizabeth, Margie, Emma, Bo, and Nelle. (Courtesy of Emma Walton.)

With the explosion of growth in the Research Triangle in the 1980s, Morrisville found itself enveloped by a number of rapidly growing communities, such as Cary. When the town celebrated its 150th anniversary, it could rightly claim to have become the "Heart of the Triangle." (Courtesy of Morrisville Town Archives.)

In 2002, Mayor Gordon Cromwell (far left) and (from left to right) commissioners Thad Conrad, Peter Martin, Jan Faulkner, and Liz Johnson pose in historic costumes as part of Morrisville's 150th anniversary celebration, commemorating the town's founding in 1852. (Courtesy of Morrisville Town Archives.)

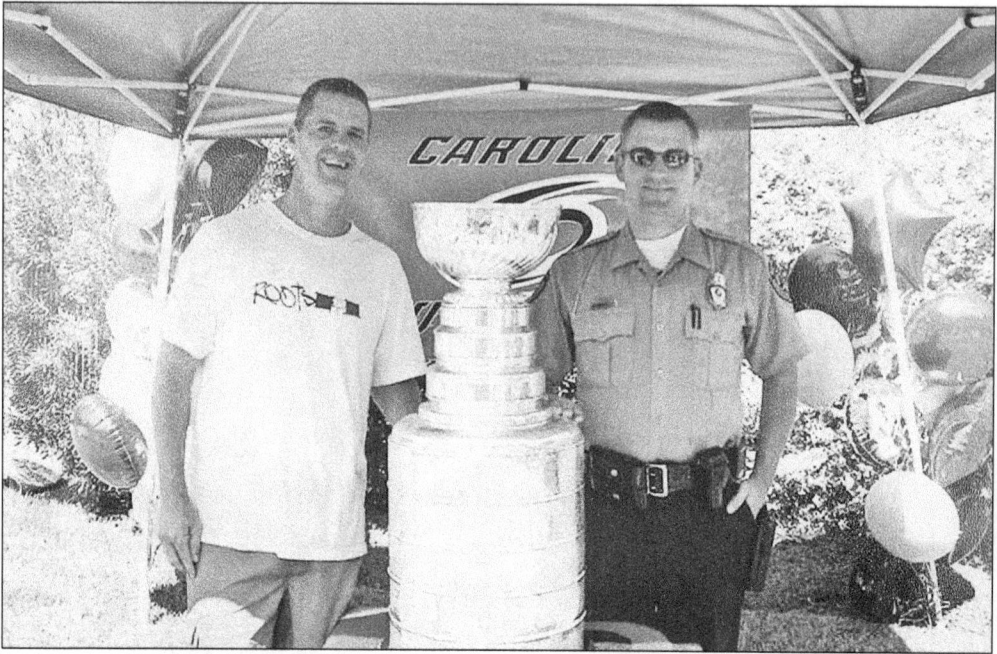

Sgt. Carlos Sanchez of the Morrisville Police Department poses with an assistant coach and former player of the Carolina Hurricanes, Jeff Daniels, after the team won the Stanley Cup hockey championship in 2006. The town officially presented them with a key to the city. The Hurricanes opened their first offices in Morrisville in 1997. (Courtesy of Morrisville Town Archives.)

In 2006, a historic marker honoring the Shiloh community was dedicated. (Photograph by the author.)

Morrisville's past meets the future as town planner Ben Hitchings, in hat, and development consultants chat with the town's oldest citizen, Mary Page Ferrell, during the town's revitalization project in 2006. (Courtesy of Morrisville Town Archives.)

Visit us at
arcadiapublishing.com

www.ingramcontent.com/pod-product-compliance
Lightning Source LLC
Chambersburg PA
CBHW050702110426
42813CB00007B/2063